INDIAN WISDOM AND ITS
GUIDING POWER

D0800818

INDIAN WISDOM
AND ITS
GUIDING POWER

Brad & Sherry Steiger

A Division of Schiffer Publishing
4880 Lower Valley Rd.
Atglen, PA 19310 USA

Cover Artwork by S.W. Ferguson.

Elements of the cover illustration:
North star and five stationary stars represent the six spirits of the world. Falling star and magpie
bird from the Ghost dancers' legend. Symbols of the guardian bird of the sky and "star spirits" of
the dead warriors who return to earth as shooting stars. Turtle spirit of the earth god. Six eagle
feathers, symbol of the wind spirit. Bear tooth necklace, symbol of bravery and knowledge. Red,
yellow, blue prayer "rainbow" shawl-blanket. Lightning snake, symbol of fire and light. Butterfly,
from Aztec and Apache lore. Represents magic and beauty from the god of children and laughter.

ISBN: 0-924608-129

Printed in United States of America

Published by Whitford Press
A Division of Schiffer Publishing, Ltd.
4880 Lower Valley Road
Atglen, PA 19310 USA
Phone: (610) 593-1777 Fax: (610) 593-2002
E-mail: schifferbk@aol.com
Please visit our web site catalog at
www.schifferbooks.com
or write for a free catalog.
This book may be purchased from the publisher.
Please include $3.95 postage.
Try your bookstore first.

In Europe, Schiffer books are distributed by
Bushwood Books
6 Marksbury Avenue
Kew Gardens
Surrey TW9 4JF England
Phone: 44 (0)181 392-8585;
Fax: 44 (0)181 392-9876
E-mail: Bushwd@aol.com

Please try your bookstore first.
We are interested in hearing from authors
with book ideas on related subjects.

CONTENTS

Chapter One

WALK THE PATH
OF THE SHAMAN

There is an enormous amount of archetypal power and energy to be gained from an exploration of American Indian Medicine. Today, throughout North America, Canada, Great Britain, Europe, and Japan, men and women have come to the exciting realization that they can use Medicine Power to receive profound insights into how they may best deal with the modern world.

Yes, as contradictory as that may seem, these ancient techniques speak as well to *today* as they did to *yesterday* – and what is more, they open the door to a more productive and empowered *tomorrow*.

As we share knowledge of Indian Medicine, we will also share some of the wisdom of our Amerindian Shaman friends and teachers, such as Rolling Thunder, Sun Bear, Grandfather David, Chief Eagle, Twylah Nitsch and others, as well as some of the insights that we ourselves have gained on our own search for meaning and balance. We agree with the Medicine Priests' conviction that <u>now</u> is the time to reveal certain of the ancient and guarded truths.

The focus of this book is on the empowerment of the individual reader. We will emphasize the universality of medicine power and illustrate its practical applications with personal exercises that have been carefully designed to enable the reader to go within and find the balance and the strength of the "wise ones." The inner wisdom of the knowing elders is desperately needed in our world of separation and discord!

DISCOVER YOUR INNER POWER
AND BALANCE

The study of American Indian Medicine will in no way compromise your present faith or spiritual expression. On the contrary, an understanding of this power system will help to illumine whatever your path and will aid you in achieving a greater comprehension of your goals and your true mission on Earth.

There is only one Source, one God, one Great Spirit; all men are brothers, all women are sisters, and all those who achieve an attitude of humility, a respect for all living things, a sense of harmony with their environment, a balance between the sacred and the mundane, may reach out and touch the Great Mystery and receive its strength. However, because of cultural differences, we apprehend the Great Mystery in various ways, and we receive the sacred transfer of its universal energy in different symbols.

The old ways and the ancient traditions have always been carefully nurtured and quietly cherished, but Medicine Power has now returned in a manner that reveals our Amerindian heritage as laden with spiritual insights fraught with special meaning for our new age of ever-rising awareness.

The sacrificial blood that was spilled has begun to dry. Collective guilt has given way to expanding consciousness and produced a generation that may at last be willing to give peace and love a chance.

Today the essential self within each human may be explored without apology, and thoughtful men and women are able to see that the psychoreligious system of Amerindian Medicine was centuries ahead of the white man's psychology. The shamans, the sacred priests, had explored inner space to an extent not even dreamed of by the invaders who crushed the red man with death and debasement.

Dr. Walter Houston Clark, Professor Emeritus of Andover Newton Theological Seminary, gave this answer to the question of why there is such current interest in the teachings of Indian medicine:

"I think our civilization has overemphasized the rational faculties of man. Our ideas of science have been so restrictive that the essential nature of human beings is being starved.

"Unconsciously, modern man is reaching out for something that goes beyond the purely rational, the purely scientific. Our young people especially are ready for an expression of the intuitive side of life."

Although many may cry out in their need for such wisdom, the great

Cherokee medicine priest Rolling Thunder warns that without the proper guidance very few can survive the challenge of walking softly on Mother Earth. Rolling Thunder calls those who learn to walk in balance, the "Thunder People," those who will "put things back together in their proper order."

In Rolling Thunder's cosmology, "The power of healing is the same as the power of love."

Sun Bear, a Chippewa Medicine Priest, lectures worldwide to audiences who are eager for his instructions on how to become self-reliant and his message that "knowledge *is* healing."

"If a person can find better balance within self," Sun Bear says, "then that *is* healing."

Mohawk medicine practitioner Rarihokwats defined the power of Amerindian medicine in these words:

"It is the power of creation. Whatever that power is, it causes the grass to grow, the Earth to rotate. This is a tremendous power. It is the power to create life. And the more that Indian people or other people become acquainted with that power, the more they are able to internalize and use and flow with that power.

The power is also the recognition that you are a part of nature and that everything is part of one whole. You are not only a part of the whole, but the whole is part of you."

Rarihokwats made an excellent point when he told us that non-Indian people should not simply copy the Indians' application of medicine power, but that they should develop their own medicine in the same way that Indian people had developed this power:

"Go to the waters and listen. Try to hear what it is that the waters have to say. What is the essence of the spirit of the waters? The only formula is to go and sit and listen.

Dr. Walter Huston Clark assures us that the willingness to receive insights from ancient tradition is not a step backwards, intellectually or spiritually: "I think that the Indians have enormous contributions to make in their religious traditions and in their attitude toward the environment. I don't think we need to turn the clock back two or three hundred years, but I do believe that in our metaphysics we have much to learn from the Indians."

"Sometime ago I came across a statement from William James in which he says, `The mother sea and fountainhead of all religion lies in the mystical experiences of the individual. All theologies, all ecclesiasticisms are secondary growths super-imposed'."

AN INCANTATION FOR POWER

Hear the power of my voice.
My swiftness is the eagle's:
I see and hear the world over.
The bear shall obey the magic of my Medicine;
My strength lies in the Great Mystery.
I shall fear no one!
I walk among serpents;
I fear no thing!
My Medicine is strong!

THE EARTH MOTHER

According to Winnebago tradition, in ancient days the Great Spirit awakened from a long dream, and finding himself alone, removed a piece of his body near his heart, mixed it with a bit of earth, and from them, fashioned a spirit entity. Pleased with this creation, the Great Spirit gave expression to three other spirit entities in the same form. The first four created beings became the spirits of the four winds.

After the Great Spirit had enjoyed the company of these entities for a time, he decided to create a female spirit being, who was the Earth Mother. She was first without covering, with no trees, no grass. Perceiving this, the Great Spirit created a vast quantity of grasses, trees, and herbs.

After this task was completed, the Great Spirit noticed that the Earth Mother had grown irregular in her motions. He was thus obliged to create four beasts and four serpents and place them under her for support. This addition excited the four winds, who blew upon the Earth Mother so furiously that she rolled about more then ever. Seizing at last upon the final solution, the Great Spirit created a buffalo and placed it beneath the Earth Mother, thus balancing her motions and establishing harmony.

The Algonquin and various other tribes relate a similar account of creation, but it is upon the back of a great tortoise that the Earth Mother achieves her stability. Such a legend may account for the Turtle Clan being the peacemakers among the majority of Eastern forest tribes.

Among the Ottawa tribe of Indians is found the following tradition of the creation of the earth:

MESSENGER WOLF

> When the earth, which was found in the claws and in the mouth of the muskrat, began to expand itself upon the surface of the water, The Great Spirit sat, day by day, watching its enlargement.
>
> When he was no longer able to see the extent of it, he sent out a wolf, and told him to run around the ground, and then to return to him, that he might thus know how large it had become.
>
> The wolf was absent only a short time, and returned. After some time the Great Spirit sent the wolf out a second time with similar directions, and he was gone two years. Again, after this, he sent him out, and he returned no more. Then the Great Spirit gave the younger brothers, the animals, each his peculiar food. He instructed those animals which were to be food for men, that they should not resist but permit themselves to be slain, as long as the method of killing was a merciful one.

The mythmakers of certain Mexican tribes portrayed Cihuacohuatl, the Great Serpent Woman, to be the mother of the human race. Originally the mother of two sons, who entered into a situation of strife similar to that of Cain and Abel, she bore other children in an effort to procreate increased harmony among humankind.

The most common term for the essence of the earth spirit among the various tribes was Great or Grand Mother – which has evolved into the currently popular Earth Mother – and the most frequent emblem associated with her was the tortoise. Cross-culturally, the ancient Chinese also regarded the tortoise, supporter of the earth, as one of four supernatural animals that presided over the destinies of the Empire. (The three others were the stag [guardian of literature], the Phoenix [guardian of virtue], and the dragon [guardian of national authority].)

The tortoise was also sacred to the Greek God Hermes. In the sacred books of the Hindus, Vishnu, in the form of a tortoise, is represented as bearing up the earth in the abyss of waters.

THE GREAT MYSTERY

The late Dallas Chief Eagle was a masterful spiritual warrior of his people. On his father's side, he was a descendant of the great Chief Red Cloud of the Teton Sioux [Lakota]; on his mother's side, he was descended from Crazy Horse, perhaps the greatest of mystic warriors. Chief Eagle once said that the Lakota never employed one special symbol for the Great Spirit, the Great Mystery, because ". . . .the Indian never sat around trying to figure out what the Great Spirit looked like."

A symbol for the Great Spirit that might find some kind of general approval among Indians, Chief Eagle mused, might be the symbol of peace, the pipe, or the crossed pipes, with stems upward. The pipe is one of the most powerful of symbols in all tribes. In the 1920s, Francis La Flesche, in his study of the Osage tribe, suggested that the several parts of the pipe were spoken of as if they were parts of the warrior himself. At the same time, each man was also representative of the tribe as a whole and as an aspect of the Sky Father and the Earth Mother by which he is surrounded. Here, condensed form La Flesche's paraphrase of the chant [Vol. IX, No.2, of *Art and Archaeology*], are words as solemn and meaningful to the Medicine practitioner as are the utterances of the priest during the celebration of Mass:

> Behold, this pipe. Verily a man!
> Within it I have placed my being.
> Place within it your own being, also,
> Then free shall you be from all that brings death.
>
> Behold, the neck of the pipe!
> Within it I have placed my own neck.

The pipe was an integral element in the making of Medicine for many tribes. This Plains Indian pipe, circa late 1800s, has a catlinite bowl and quillwork on the stem.

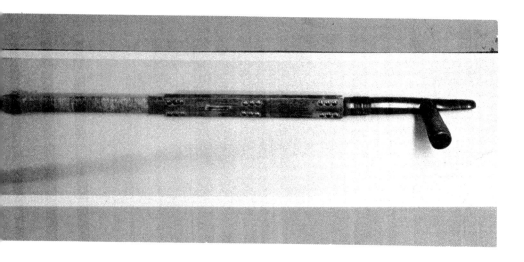

Place within it your neck, also,
Then free shall you be from all that brings death!

Behold, the mouth of the pipe!
Within it I have placed my own mouth.
Place within it your mouth, also,
Then free shall you be from all that brings death!

Behold, the hollow of the pipe!
Within it I have placed the hollow of my own body.
Place within it the hollow of your own body, also,
Then shall you be free from all that brings death!

Behold, the thong that holds together the bowl
and the stem!
Within it I have placed my breathing-tube.
Place within it your own breathing-tube, also,
Then shall you be free from all that brings death!

When you turn from the rising sun to the setting sun to go
against your enemies,
This pipe shall you use when you go forth to invoke aid
from [the Great Mystery],
Then shall your prayers be speedily granted,
Yea, even before the sun shall o'er-top the walls
of your dwelling,
Your prayers shall surely be granted!

Wakan, a word some authorities often cite as the "name" of the Great Spirit, is, according to the Lakota and Dakota people, better translated as "holy, sacred."

"We pay homage to this Great Spirit – or Great Mystery – through his creations – the Sun, the Earth, the Wind, the Thunder, the Lightning," Chief Eagle explained. "The Earth must never be spoiled by the men who worship in mere lodges, by the arrogance of men who have never known defeat, by the self-righteousness of those who violate treaties and punish those who would resist such violations."

The Great Mystery made nature for humankind to use and to preserve. "But nature also imposes obligations upon us," he continued. "We are only passing through life on our way to the Spirit World of our ancestors."

There is a traditional saying that states the following:

"There are many worlds – some that have passed, some that are to come. In one, we creep; in another, we walk; in another, we fly.

"The bad men will always swim as the fish or creep like the serpents."

A death-chant from long ago recites the reminder of humankind's common fate: "Let all mourn and weep. Oh, weep for the dead. Think of the dead lying in the grave. We shall die soon. Oh, let sorrow melt your hearts. Let your tears flow fast. We are all one people. We are all friends. All our hearts are one heart."

Dallas Chief Eagle worked hard at creating open lines of communication between the native people and their unruly guests on this continent. "We Indians pray to the Holy Mystery and ask that some day the whitemen will better understand us, that the needs of their consciousness will awake and grow. Our freedom is our way of life, but to others, it could be a difficult thing. You have to know who you are in order to feel the Great Spirit in nature. It is only through nature that one can gain communion with the Holy Mystery."

WHAT MAKES INDIAN MEDICINE WORK?

In the modern classic *Black Elk Speaks*, John G Neihardt tells of accompanying the aged holy man of the Oglala Sioux to Harney Peak, the same place where the spirits had taken Black Elk in a vision when he had been young. The old man painted himself as he had seen himself in his great vision and called out to the Great Spirit to hear his prayer that the Indian people might once again find their way back into the sacred hoop, the Great Circle.

Neihardt writes that, as they stood by and watched, thin clouds began to gather out of a clear sky. "A scant chill rain began to fall and there was low, muttering thunder without lightning. With tears running down [his] cheeks, [Black Elk] raised his voice to a thin high wail, and chanted: `In sorrow I am sending a feeble voice, O Six Powers of the World. Hear me in my sorrow, for I may never call again. O make my people live!'"

According to Neihardt, Black Elk stood for a few minutes in silence, his face uplifted, weeping in the rain. Soon, the sky was once again cloudless.

What makes Amerindian Medicine Power work? How can sacred doctors summon wind, and squeeze rain out of cloudless skies?

"Some people would think of these things as magic," Sun Bear commented. "We think of them as simple, using forces that have been here for all time for the benefit of our needs. Magic is not magic if you understand it. It is something that works. It is when you will something into existence because you have need of it.

"Knowledge never changes; it remains a strong and continuing thing," Sun Bear continued. "Indian medicine and the power behind it is very much alive today. It has not vanished; it is not antiquated. To the traditional Indian people, we see more of a strong need for it today than ever before. We see a continent being devastated by people who are stupidly trying to get rich quick by raping the Earth Mother. We feel that it is basic for the survival of this nation that people learn much of our traditions, much of the knowledge that we have to teach.

"I regard myself as a humanitarian. I love my fellowman – Indian, black or white or whatever. Those whom I call brothers are those who share the same philosophy and respect for the Earth Mother and for each other as human beings.

"We traditional people consider ourselves keepers and protectors of the Earth Mother. We have a responsibility not only to this generation, but to all generations to come. That is why we are concerned over the environment, concerned over the natural resources. We feel that in other lands across the world, there are other people of ancient origin who have labored in a manner similar to our work – people who are keepers and protectors."

Attempting a rigid definition of Medicine Power concepts or a simple explanation of the Indian's understanding of the Great Mystery most often meets with rebuke among the serious Medicine practitioners.

"Dogmas!" Chief Eagle scowled, his voice almost a growl. "Who dares create dogmas? How can anyone say what the Great Spirit thinks? The Supreme Power gives man a message, sets an example.

"The Great Mystery sets forth guidelines. If any man puts forth any dogma or doctrine, I think he has put forth a challenge to the Great Spirit!

"Let those who mock Medicine practice experience it. It is an insult to the Great Mystery to discard its message in favor of following a human's created dogma."

QUESTIONS FOR SELF-EVALUATION

Are you comfortable with the concept of God, the Great Spirit, as "the Great Mystery," a force that is present in all things?

Do you feel that such a concept is compatible or incompatible with previous beliefs which you may hold?

Think of the belief structures of your closest friends or of your family members. How do you think they would respond to Chief Eagle's comments about dogmas and doctrines?

What is your inner feeling about nature and your sense of responsibility toward its various manifestations and creatures?

Do you have an awareness of the daily violations to the ecosystem of the Earth Mother? When you read of the destruction of the rain forests, the pollutions of our rivers, lakes, and streams, the damage being done to the ozone layer, do you feel a personal sense of violation and injury? Or do you have complete confidence in the scientists and politicians to look after our welfare? Are you willing to trust the Future to others? Or do you wish to assume a personal interaction with the Earth Mother and assume some measure of personal responsibility for the collective future of the planet and its people?

WORDS OF CAUTION TO THOSE WHO WOULD FOLLOW THE PATH OF THE SHAMAN

Brazilian shaman Antonio Costa e Silva in an interview given to Arianna Siegel in the Mid-Summer, 1989 issue of *SHAMAN'S DRUM*, shares advice for people starting on a shamanic path:

"Don't start! More seriously, my advice is `don't play' with shamanism. Sometimes we don't see the effect of the powers we invoke and play with – but results come nevertheless. You can request things for your own happiness; that's fine; but don't try techniques just for fun, and don't try to learn things without being prepared. The effect of such actions could trap you for a long, long time on the astral plane, and it could take many incarnations to clean up what you do.

"One problem in America is the belief that shamanism or spirituality can be acquired through workshops. But it isn't so. Shamanism is the will of life, the way of life – it is part of you. There's little faith here in the United States because people think teachings can be bought, and buying doesn't develop faith."

"In my culture you can't buy teachings for money. People often devote their lives to a practice before they receive teachings or benefits. But here, once people pay money for workshops, they expect teachers to give them teachings and empowerment, even if they aren't ready to receive them."

Costa e Silva's words are sound and wise. They were virtually the same words we heard from our friend, Kuichy, an apprentice shaman who was our guide through some of the ruins and secrets of Peru – an incredible and powerful journey which we undertook in September 1990. The seriousness of involvement, commitment, and discipline has been emphasized to us by the powerful inter-tribal Medicine shaman, Rolling Thunder, and by Sun Bear, a sacred Chippewa Medicine Priest, as well as by many others. It is in this same spirit that we offer this book on Shamanism to you, that you may have a better understanding of some profound teachings and ways which can be applied to your inner life with outer results – if you are sincere.

Shamanism cannot be learned during a three-day or a three-week intensive or by reading a special book or a hundred books. Shamanism is a commitment for life!

Costa e Silva warns, "You can go to many places and reap benefits; that's fine, but when you decide that your path is to be a shaman, then you should start to look for a teacher on the right path. Look at the teacher of the teacher, the teacher of that teacher, and at the teachings of the tradition."

The Brazilian shaman declares that true shamans are those who can totally open their hearts to another's suffering and work to transform that suffering into love and compassion. It is our hope and prayer that we may each move closer to that goal.

It seems that for some years now, people have been saying that the stresses in and on their lives have never been greater. Daily, if not minute by minute, as time ticks away deeper into the purification at hand – and the Great Purification around the corner – more and more stresses are added. In each of our lives we have an increasing personal need for peace, healing, and love – and a wish for peace, healing, and love for this planet, Mother Earth. Some of us have an intense desire not just to experience these things, but to contribute and to do whatever possible to bring these about.

It is our belief that the most powerful things one can do to change the world is to understand and to change the beliefs that one has about the nature of self... life... others... reality and then to accomplish something more positive and begin to act according to those new beliefs.

The true nature of life is perfection, harmony, order, and balance. To understand the nature of life, its energy, its Source, its resources, and the *inner* - relationship and *inter* - relationship of the environment and the impact of our thoughts on same, can help us realize the impact of human decisions on these relationships. Then we can effectively move into positive action, healing, and growth.

This we believe is a most important journey, a quest to connect our past, our present, and our future. The path of the shaman in the traditional native American belief construct centers around life in harmony and in balance. The teachings and exercises, the wisdom and guidance from the many shamans that we share with you are for that purpose and toward that end – which is the beginning!

THE NARROW PATH OF THE INITIATE

The path that the initiate must follow to become a shaman is a narrow one, involving many obstacles and trials necessary for self-cleansing. The path of purification is the path of overcoming.

Initiation has been explained by some shamans as taking place in our lives in many ways and at many times. Initiation is essentially the acknowledgement of an awakened conscience on the part of one who has made a conscious decision at some point in life to become a seeker of truth and to take as many steps as necessary to achieve that end.

Initiation may occur in meditation, in profound dreams – or while doing the laundry. Such an awakening is not necessarily a sign of spiritual development, but represents a willingness and a readiness to help humankind and Mother Earth. It is but the beginning.

To be chosen by a Shaman as an initiate or an apprentice shaman is very much like having the "call" to become a Christian minister. Very often there is a "born again" experience and a kind of baptism, as well as a cleansing of oneself from the past in order to embark on the road of a greater commitment and responsibility. There is an inherent obligation on the part of the initiate to share whatever seeds of truth were received and to assist others to achieve insights into a higher purpose.

It is said that the burden and struggle would be much greater and more difficult if the knowledge gained should be *mis*used rather than *not* used, so when you make the decision to choose the path of initiation, be certain that you are ready.

The mere process of learning from the shamanic wisdoms and traditions does not require the process of initiation. The true shaman reviews all life as interdependent and considers that we are all caretakers of it. Shamans encourage all people to care for one another, ourselves, the Earth Mother, and all things that live on her. One certainly need not be either an initiate or a shaman to assume such responsibility.

MAKING SPIRITUAL "FOOTPRINTS"

The mystery of individual identity as it struggles for expression against the vastness of Time and the Cosmos is nowhere better vocalized than in the corn-planting chant of the Osage women as they tamp the hilled kernels and sing the wonder of their own bodily magic. (Again we are indebted to Francis La Flesche, this time from his report to the Bureau of American Ethnology, 1925):

> Footprints I have made; a sacred act.
> Footprints I have made; to lie in even lines.
> Footprints I have made; they are broken.
> Footprints I have made; in which stand leafy stalks.
> Footprints I have made; the leaves wave in the wind.
> Footprints I have made; the ears cross in profusion.
> Footprints I have made; I pluck the ears....
> Footprints I have made; there is joy in my house.

THE ELEMENTS OF MEDICINE POWER

A crucial element in the spiritual chemistry that comprises medicine power is the ability to rise above linear time. The conventional concept of time existing in some sort of sequential stream flowing along in one dimension is totally inadequate to provide us with a full assessment of reality. This one, two, three kind of time may be convenient when we are in an ordinary, conscious, waking state, since it will limit the input of sensory data and allow us to deal effectively with the "present." But our essential selves have the ability to rise to a level of consciousness wherein past, present, and future form an Eternal now and wherein we may gain access to this level of consciousness in dreams and in visions.

In his text for Ira Moskowitz' book of drawings, *American Indian Ceremonial Dances*, John Collier comments upon the Indian's possession of a time sense that is different, and happier, than the whiteman's:

> . . .Once our white race had it, too, and then the mechanized world took it away from us... We think, now, that any other time than linear, chronological time is an escapist dream. The Indians tell us otherwise, and their message and demonstration addresses itself to one of our deepest distresses and most forlorn yearnings. . . .

> . . .In solitary, mystical experience many of [us] do enter
> another time dimension. But under the frown of clockwork
> time which claims the world, we place our experience out in
> an eternity beyond the years and beyond the stars. Not out
> there did the other time dimension originate, in racial history,
> but within the germ plasm and the organic rhythms and the
> social soul; nor is its reference only or mainly to the moveless
> eternity. It is life's instinct and environment, and human soci-
> ety's instinct and environment. To realize it or not realize it
> makes an enormous difference, even a decisive difference.
> The Indians realize it, and they can make us know.

The traditional Indian sees the work of the Great Mystery in every expression of life upon the Earth Mother. Such a reverence for his environment convinced the whiteman that the Amerindian was given to the
worship of idols and graven images, a primitive man confused and
frightened by a hierarchy of many gods.

The American Indian traditionalist believes that the Great Mystery
may express Itself in many ways and may appear in a variety of forms
during the vision quest. The traditionalist also believes that the essence
of the Great Mystery's power flows through all living things. But the
Amerindian believes in only one Supreme Being. Regrettably, only a
few of the early white Americans were able to discern the distinction
between witnessing God's work in all of life and worshiping elemental
nature forces.

The most essential elements of Medicine Power appear to be the
following:

> 1.) The vision quest, with its emphasis on self-denial and
> spiritual discipline, extended to a lifelong pursuit of wisdom
> of body and soul.

> 2.) A reliance upon one's personal visions and dreams to
> provide one's direction on the path of life.

> 3.) A search for personal songs to enable one to attune
> oneself to the primal sound, the cosmic vibration of the Great
> Mystery.

> 4.) A belief in a total partnership with grandfathers and
> grandmothers who have changed planes of existence.

> 5.) The possession of a non-linear time sense.

> 6.) A receptivity to the evidence that the essence of the
> Great Mystery may be found in everything.

> 7.) A reverence and a passion for the Earth Mother, the
> awareness of one's place in the web of life, and one's responsi-
> bility toward all plant and animal life.

8.) A total commitment to one's beliefs that pervades every aspect of one's life and enables one truly to walk in balance.

GROWING IN GREATER BALANCE WITH THE EARTH MOTHER

Here is a simple, but very effective, exercise for helping you to grow in greater balance with the Earth Mother and in greater harmony with the energies of nature. It would be wonderful if you could perform this little ritual while you are walking in the woods, climbing a mountain trail, or standing by the ocean; but by giving a bit of energy to your Inner Shaman, you can work wonders in an apartment in the largest of cities.

Take a deep breath, just a comfortable, deep breath and hold it for the count of three. . . .then release it. Repeat this process three times.

Begin to look toward the North. Let your head move slowly toward the North, then lock in on the direction you know to be due North. Let your vision extend to the far, far horizon of the North. Begin to feel yourself growing taller as you look toward the North.

Now visualize yourself stretching upward, as if you are, perhaps, a tall redwood tree. Stretch your arms out in front of you as if they were limbs stretching forth.

Imagine that you can touch the far horizon of the North. Imagine that your arms are able to stretch out and touch the horizon. *Feel* your fingertips brushing the very farthest reaches of the horizon. *Feel* your arms stretching out to permit your fingertips to brush the very farthest point of the North horizon.

Visualize yourself beginning to move slowly around. *Feel* your fingertips lightly touching a forest. . .a cloud. . .an ocean. . .the waters of a lake. . .the grasses of a rolling plain.

You are turning slowly around so that your outstretched arms can move from the horizon of the North to the horizons of the West. . .the South. . .the East.

Whatever you touch – forests. . .clouds. . .streams. . .grasses – as you turn slowly around counterclockwise with your great outstretched arms, you are letting the Earth Mother know that you are aware of her. Wherever you touch, as your great arms stretch from horizon to horizon, you are blessing the Earth Mother. You are blessing her and all that you touch.

Feel the energy moving out from you, blessing all that you touch, all that you feel. And now feel the blessing returning to you from the Earth Mother.

Keep your eyes open as you move counterclockwise. Feel your fingertips brush the farthest reaches that you can see with your eyes. As far as you can see with your eyes, touch with your finger tips.

Now close your eyes. Close your eyes and know that you have become an important focal point. There is the great Earth Mother all around you. There is the great Sky Father above you. And both above and below, you sense energies, seen and unseen, felt and only guessed at.

You, through your mind, constitute the focal point that touches the universe, and caresses the Earth Mother. Open all of your senses to receive the blessing that the Earth Mother sends back to you. Feel and know yourself to be the center of a great benevolent energy, which is consecrated by all that surrounds you.

A TREE INCANTATION TO GAIN STRENGTH

O Tree, Strong tree, Chief of many of your kind,
I embrace you.
O Tall Chief,
Take thou this weakness of my back;
Give me strength instead.
Take thou this weakness of my arms;
Give me strength instead.
Let me be as thou art, strong and enduring.
Let me be as upright as thyself,
Standing between the Sky Father above,
And the Earth Mother below.
Let me be secure from storm,
And blessed in every limb.
Ho!

A PRAYER FOR WISDOM OF NATURE

O Great Spirit, bring to our white brothers and sisters the wisdom of Nature and the knowledge that if her laws are obeyed this land will again flourish and grasses and trees will grow as before. Guide those that through their councils seek to spread the wisdom of their leaders to all people. Heal the raw wounds in the earth and restore to our soil the richness which strengthens men's bodies and makes them wise in their councils. Bring to all the knowledge that great cities live only through the bounty of the good earth beyond their paved streets and towers of stone and steel. [Jasper Saunkeah, Cherokee]

A SONG FROM A PUEBLO CORN DANCE

For even while I call myself poor,
Somewhere far off
Is one who is my father.
Beseeching the breath of the divine one. . .
His life-giving breath,
His breath of old age,
His breath of waters,
His breath of seeds,. . .
His breath of fecundity,
His breath of power,
His breath of strong spirit,
His breath of all good fortune whatsoever,
Asking for his breath
And into my warm body drawing his breath,
I add to your breath
That happily you may always live.

To this end, my fathers, my children:
May you be blessed with light.

A PRAYER OF THANKSGIVING TO THE GREAT SPIRIT

Twylah Nitsch, a descendent of the brilliant Seneca orator Chief Red Jacket, once answered a request for a prayer that might be offered to the Great Mystery in a correct attitude of thanksgiving, rather than supplication, with these beautiful words:

O Great Spirit, I awake to another sun,
Grateful for gifts bestowed, granted one by one.
Grateful for the greatest gift, the precious breath of life.
Grateful for abilities to guide me day and night.
As I walk my chosen path of lessons I must learn,
Spiritual peace and happiness, rewards of life I learn.
Thank you for your spiritual strength, and for my thoughts
to pray;
Thank you for your infinite love that guides me through
the day.

Chapter Two

RECEIVE STRENGTH AND POWER FROM YOUR VISION QUEST

CHANT OF A TETON SIOUX WHO SETS OUT ON A VISION QUEST

Friends!
In ordinary life, the customs are many.
Friends!
Such ways do not interest me!
I have said it.

Dallas Chief Eagle remarked that there were quite a few people going on vision quests in the spring and the fall. On his reservation alone, there were six of them out at one time:

There are different levels of vision quests. Sometimes you can just go for a walk and meditate so that you can get close to nature. There is a strength in tranquility and peace. They provide energy.

If one wishes to go on the full vision quest, complete with fasting and the seeking of a guide and a vision, he walks in the footsteps of the saints throughout history who have communicated with God, the Great Spirit. The biblical figures did it; the Indians do it.

I think the mind can be made to absorb itself and expand itself. I think one can do intense meditation, and I think one can cultivate this ability. I concentrate intensely on a subject. I assume no special body position. I take careful pains to guard against being disturbed. I've tried to meditate in forests and beside streams where there was too much interference. I must reach an area of complete solitude. If one gains a proper avenue for introspection, the mind absorbs itself – then explodes, bringing knowledge to the seeker.

I think this knowledge comes from a higher power. Sometimes when you speak in this area, you lose a lot when you use the term "God." You may lose proper perspective of a subject that has become so associated in our society with Christianity that God is considered only from that point of view.

I think there are levels of power and intelligence, and I believe you can reach a definite higher level of energy through meditation and intense concentration. I don't think it takes the mind long to grow accustomed to rising to higher levels and to learn how to gain proper knowledge from different levels of energy and power. I think it is quite possible to train the mind to reach these unknown dimensions.

Chief Eagle had these suggestions for one about to begin the quest:

First, I would tell the seeker to cleanse himself spiritually. Take a sweat bath. After this, don't touch any food. You may drink some water.

Go somewhere where you will have a minimum of interference. Then, sitting, kneeling, or standing, meditate. Think on why you are there.

Between a day and a half to three days – I should say within four days – the message will come. The message may be received in English or in some other language, but you will understand it, the entire concept.

Or you might receive the message in the form of a chant. In ancient times, Indians sang their prayers, because they felt singing was of a higher order than ordinary speech.

THE PERSONAL GUIDING FORCE OF THE VISION QUEST

The personal revelatory experience received during the vision quest becomes the fundamental guiding force in any traditional Amerindian's Medicine Power. The dogma of tribal rituals and the religious expressions of others become secondary to the guidance one receives from his personal visions.

The vision quest is basic to all native North American religious experience, but one may certainly see similarities between the proud Indian youth presenting himself to the Great Spirit as helpless, shelterless, and humble, and the supplicants of Western occultism and Medieval Christianity fasting, flagellating, and prostrating themselves in mo-

Dallas Chief Eagle, Teton Sioux

nastic cells. In Christianity, of course, the questing mystic kneels before a personal deity and beseeches insight from God, whom he hopes to please with his examples of piety and self-sacrifice. In Amerindian Medicine, the power, the *mana*, granted by the vision quest comes from a vast and impersonal repository of spiritual energy; and each recipient of Medicine Power becomes his own priest, his own shaman, who will be guided by guardian spirits and by insights into the workings of the Cosmos granted to him by visions sent from the Great Spirit.

To emphasize the uniqueness of the vision quest as the fundamental guiding force in Amerindian Medicine is to underscore certain universal aspects of the experience and to invite comparisons with the *samadhi* of the Yogi, the *satori* of the Zen Buddhist, Dr. Raymond Bucke's Cosmic Consciousness, and the *ecstasy* of the Christian mystic. In the chapter "Basic Mystical Experience" in his *Watcher on the Hills*, Dr. Raynor C. Johnson named seven characteristics of illumination which we list, together with comments directed toward our analysis of the vision quest of the Amerindian:

1.) *The Appearance of Light*. One instantly thinks of Paul (ne' Saul) on the road to Damascus being struck blind by the sudden appearance of a bright light, but the guardian spirit also manifests as a light being.

2.) *Ecstasy, Love, Bliss*. The traditional Amerindian, stereotypically regarded as stoical and unfeeling, regards the vision quest as a supreme emotional experience.

3.) *The Approach to Oneness*. The very essence of the traditional way of life is the awareness that one is a part of the Universe and the Universe is a part of him.

4.) *Insights Given*. Not only does the seeker receive valuable insights and a guardian, but he receives a secret name.

5.) *Effect on Health and Vitality*. After the illumination experience, the percipient – although he may have fasted for several days and may have depleted his physical strength through monotonous tasks designed to quiet his conscious mind – will feel invigorated and will walk back to the council in full stride to recount his vision.

6.) *Sense of Time Obscured*. This seems less dramatic to the traditional Amerindian than to other recipients of illumination, since he has never permitted himself to become enslaved by linear time.

7.) *Effects on Living*. The receiving of the personal vision serves as the traditional Indian's support throughout his entire life and is incorporated into his world-view with total commitment.

Sun Bear said that he did not go on his actual vision quest until he was in his twenties: "Before the coming of my realization of what I must do with my life, I spent much time seeking my direction and learning from accomplished Medicine people. I spent time with the Hopis, the Navahos, and many other tribes, and I gained respect for their Medicine. Since those days, Medicine has come to me at different times and in different ways.

"One time I was on top of a mountain when I received a vision of an earthquake. The next day I called a friend in Los Angeles, and things had happened as I had seen them in my vision.

"Some things that I see, I cannot always tell my people, because they are not yet ready. I know of certain shortcuts to get to where we have to go. In Medicine, some things are of value to yourself personally. Some Medicine people have power chants which can be passed down and used by only one family.

"I use my dreams in many ways. I use them as a sense of warning to advise my brothers and sisters against danger. I use dreams to give me ideas to develop later."

PLAINS INDIAN SONG OF ENDURANCE

A Lone Wolf I am...
I roam in many places...
I am weary.

Twylah Nitsch said that she could "get off the world" very easily:

"I put spiritual protection around everyone, and then I place it around myself so there is complete balance. All the spiritual forces are opened up so they can circulate and everything goes in balance.

"When one is in the process of learning," Twylah explained, "the material world can be so pronounced that the student leans in the direction of worldliness. The spiritual self does not come through because it is being shut off. In order for the spiritual light to function the way it should, the teacher has to do something drastic to make the student stop what he is doing wrong and get him back to the real thing – learning about himself and his environment.

"The moment you are born, you breathe in the breath of life, the most important gift of the material world; but prior to birth, you have been endowed with the spiritual light. The spiritual light lives within the fetus. When you're born and you are dunked in the clear spring water to take your first breath, you receive the gift of life, which will help you in the world of material evolution."

Twylah Nitsch, Repositor of Seneca Wisdom.

Twylah as a young woman, already firmly on the Medecine Path.

The adoption ceremony wherein Brad Steiger became an honorary member of the Wolf Clan of the Seneca tribe. Twylah Nitsch served as his adoptive mother.

Twylah issued these words of advice to the sincere seeker:

> In order to ensure solitude, one should practice visualizing a spiritual circle around himself. This process rekindles yourself and keeps and aura close around you.
>
> The early Seneca meditated very often on how best to achieve self-improvement. He made an honest study of his personal self, both good and bad. He decided what changes he wanted to make in his personal self-pattern. He listed the personal habits he wished to establish, and he listed the personal habits he wished to break.
>
> One must always evaluate the goals which he is contemplating. Will your goals of self-improvement bring about an expansion of positive experiences?
>
> Examine your environment. Do you control your environment, or does it control you?
>
> Seek new dimensions of awareness by looking around you and discovering that which directly affects you.
>
> Tap into your creative ability and raise your highest intellectual self. Discover personal techniques whereby you might better control your gifts and abilities. Raise your perception to the unlimited level of spirituality.
>
> Your own personal symbolism can enable you to establish a focal point for meditation. If you believe that you need some kind of gimmick to aid in your self-development, don't go out and buy some tacky external thing. Discover a personal symbol that truly fits your personality.
>
> The ancient Senecas taught their children to pray at an early age. The children would pretend that they were in council. They would pray in thanksgiving. This was their first introduction to going into the Silence, seeking self-development, and offering proper prayers.
>
> The young Seneca were told to tap into their highest intellectual awareness.
>
> They were told not to force awareness. This is a passive state that must come at its own pace.
>
> They were instructed that prayer was a creative process that began with an idea. Prayer must be accompanied with feeling. This is so important. You cannot have prayer without having a definite idea accompanied with feeling.
>
> They were taught that in order to have a prayer fulfilled, it is necessary to understand the levels of feeling. This understanding must exist before the desires and actions can be controlled.

One of the first things Seneca children learned was that they might create their own world, their own environment, by visualizing actions and desires in prayer. A child will create his own world through imagery. He will create his own environment. This is a natural gift with which we are all born. The Senecas believed that everything that made life important came from within. Prayer assisted in developing a guideline toward discipline and self-control.

I am saddened by the fact that today's parents do not discipline their children on a very high spiritual level. This is so important.

SHARING THE VISION

Holy visions!
Hither come, we pray you, come unto us,
Bringing with you joy;
Come, oh, come to us, holy visions,
Bringing with you joy.

Black Elk has said, "A man who has a vision is not able to use the power of it until after he has performed the vision on earth for the people to see."

He, of course, is not talking about the highly personal insight received during the vision quest, but the great vision that will enable one to become a Medicine practitioner and have the strength to cure others and to counsel those who may come to him in need.

"Of course it was not I who cured," Black Elk qualifies in *Black Elk Speaks*. "It was the power from the other world, and the visions and ceremonies had only made me like a hole through which the power could come to the two-leggeds. If I thought that I was doing it myself, the hole would close up and no power could come through."

Black Elk's qualifying remarks sound so much like the disclaimers which we have heard from sincere psychic sensitives, mediums, and healers who refuse any personal credit for their feats, but rather refer to themselves as "channels" through which the power may flow. It appears that it may be a universal law of metaphysics that those who are chosen to serve as "holes," as "channels," be ever conscious of the proper perspective in which they are to regard the stewardship of their unique abilities.

In the timeless realm wherein you receive visions, living diagrams, thought awareness, you can understand more thoroughly your present situation, your mission on Earth. You can even perceive the future. Sometimes visions appear that symbolically explain the great mysteries of existence – the questions humankind has asked since intelligent thought first formed in the more illuminated corners of the brain.

You have the ability to enter a dimension that operates on a higher vibration, where love, wisdom, and knowledge exist and can be given to you. With practice you can transcend to the space beyond the physical realm and lead a more meaningful and productive life.

Some teachings will be given to you in words, without an accompanying vision; yet the words create thoughts that permit the mind to imagine as if a diagram accompanied it.

When you permit yourself to enter an altered state of consciousness, you must want to receive awareness, to receive a vision teaching. You must desire to be taught, so that a greater understanding of many things may then be yours. This desire must be uppermost in your heart and mind.

You will be transported to a beautiful realm where a magnificent, colorful panorama of teachings of awareness will be given to you. While you are in this realm, love will permeate your entire being. It is in this dimension that angels, masters, and guides will visibly or invisibly interact with you, share with you, teach you all that you desire to know.

What you will see must be shared, and it must not be permitted to stagnate. What you receive here and see here, *must* be shared with others.

In the sharing, you will more fully understand what you have received; and you will be able to describe it and relay it more easily. You will also receive anew. You must give to receive, just as you must give away energy before you can receive the same energy afresh, anew.

The receiving of a teaching vision comes when you are meditating, when your mind is quiet. Prayer is not meditation. Prayer is speaking, asking. Meditation is receiving, listening, waiting. If any mundane thought enters your mind, gently push it away. Never shove an intruding thought away from you. Instead, tell it that you will think of it later and gently, very gently, ease it from your mind.

With the eyes closed, most people see vague outlines or images or swirls. With practice, the images will become clearer, focused, with colors coming in and going out. Soon the colors will remain and become vivid – then all will be clear.

Meditation is an art form wherein you receive the creative energy awaiting you. Soon you will become a part of the scene of the image, and you will experience it for a time.

Next, you will find yourself freely flying through space to a particular destination that has been selected by your higher self, your soul, or perhaps by your guide, master, or teacher. When you reach this place, you will receive many awarenesses. You will feel freer than you have ever imagined. You will free yourself from the material world to which you have always been attached and step into the true reality of all that is.

Your vision teaching will come to you in a matter of minutes – ten at the very most, rarely more – though you may feel as though an hour has passed. This is a truth that appears universal; for in that domain, in the altered state of consciousness, there exists no sensation of time as we know it.

When you receive your vision teaching, a feeling of "knowing" will envelop you. You will feel that you have always known this awareness, and you will have an inner belief that what you have received is truth. You will feel it vibrate in your heart and in your stomach. No one will be able to shake you from your belief in your teaching vision.

When you tell others of your teaching, you will be able to speak beyond what you were consciously aware of at the time you received the vision. This is due to your having not only absorbed the frequencies of higher awareness that accompanied the vision teaching, but also having learned more than you were consciously aware. You have thereby been elevated in your vibrational awareness. You will be able to comprehend more than you could have understood before the vision teaching was ever received.

By telling others you will become even more aware of the entire truth than when you first envisioned it, for you can now perceive it from many sides, thus gaining different perspectives. By giving you receive in greater abundance.

GOING INTO THE SILENCE

Many Medicine Priests refer to meditation as "going into the Silence," Here is Twylah's beautifully stated explanation of that process:

> Going into the Silence meant communing with nature in spirit, mind, and body. Nature's atmosphere radiated the spirituality of the Supreme Power and provided the path that led the early Seneca into the Great Silence.
>
> The legend of the First Messenger of the Great Mystery tells of the encounter with the spiritual essence that was responsible for the practice of going into the Silence.
>
> Four very old people, two men and two women who were

endowed with great wisdom gleaned throughout their advancing years, sat in the woodlands on the warm earth near a brooklet that crept beneath a canopy of leaves and branches. They had come to reminisce of their kindred experiences when suddenly the heavens opened:

> A Glorious Beam of Light
> In All Its Brilliant Splendor
> Gently Drifted Over Them
> Seeding Peace and Solemnity
> On Everything It Touched.

They watched in wonderment, spellbound by the Light's sublime magnificence. It filtered through their bodies, cleansing them of all infirmities.

Presently, they were borne aloft to a place of divine ecstasy where the "Secret of the Ages" was revealed to them, telling of things to be. They saw the first messenger of the Supreme Power: the spiritual hand with outstretched fingers and thumb. The message was "*Ens-wy-stawg*," meaning, "It comes through." This was the first spiritual experience of "going into Silence."

The symbolism of the hand signifies that as the thumb assists the four fingers in life, unity, equality, and eternity, so does the Great Spirit assist all things in nature.

From that time on, the four people of wisdom spent their remaining days communing with nature in reverence and solitude. Their spiritual insight increased as others joined them to listen to their words of wisdom and spiritual counseling.

From this revelation the entire custom of sitting in council evolved. It became evident that the messengers of the Great Spirit wore many faces. They could be manifestations of nature, creatures, or earthy forces.

The Secret of the Ages revolved around attitudes and thoughts that instilled a sense of brotherhood with all creation. Its practice was carried on as a personal attribute in solitude with one's own thoughts in direct communication with the Creator. It mattered not when or where it was held, since the body was the chapel that housed the spiritual light.

The following procedure was found to be helpful in entering the Silence:

The Indian discovered that wherever he went he could find a stone. After selecting one of his choice, the stone was placed in the palm of the left hand with the right hand clasped on top. Holding the stone in this fashion created a union of forces within the hand. When this pulsating was felt, the Indian believed he had raised himself into the vibrational current of a higher spiritual level. The stone acted as a reminder that everything was of the same source – the spiritual brotherhood of all and everything.

The following mental procedure was also useful in entering the Silence. It helped the Indian locate a place in his mind where peace and contentment lived.

You are walking into the woods. Your feet are plotting a path on the soft, spongy ground. The path is narrow and winds around trees and bushes so that, at times, you need to duck under the low-hanging branches.

Through the clearing ahead lies a shimmering lake. The Sun spreads a rainbow of colors across the rippling surface.

Upon reaching the water's edge, you stand quietly and listen to the lapping surf, as it pushes the pebbles back and forth on the clean, warm sand. To the left is a log inviting you to sit upon its blanket of moss. You accept the invitation and settle down upon the cushioned softness, feeling it press against your body.

A breeze carrying the woodland aromas brushes your hair and caresses your face. The trees are singing the songs of nature in harmony.

The Silence majestically weaves it magic spell, as it gathers all nature within its fold. At last, the serenity of spiritual Silence flows into your every fiber, drenching it with divine purity.

You listen and *hear* the Silence.
You listen and *see* the Silence.
You listen and *smell* the Silence.
You listen and *taste* the Silence
You listen and *feel* the embrace of the Silence.

Peering through the spiritual eyes, you find the real you dwelling therein. While drifting along with the ebbing tide of spirituality, you and Nature become one, together plucking these tender moments of intimate reunion with the Supreme Power, the Great Spirit.

The Great Spirit, Divine Supreme
Maker of all and everything.
The Great Spirit, the Eternal Mind

Whose thoughts flow everlastingly.
The Great Spirit, the Master Designer
Arranger of patterns of all and everything

UNDERTAKING A GUIDED MEDITATION THAT SIMULATES THE VISION QUEST

Vision teachings are parts of a living, vibrational truth that is composed of many facets of varying levels. Depending on your personal awareness, you will see the level of truth nearest your own understanding. As you grow in awareness, you will perceive deeper levels of that very same truth, as if you are ascending a mountain that permits you to climb higher and higher. As you elevate your vibrations, rising in awareness, you will be able to achieve the highest level of consciousness; and thereby, one day see all of the very same truth.

All truth teachings appear as separate visions to our understanding, awareness, and perception. Yet they are not separate at all. They are connected one to the other, as are the images on a great tapestry.

The more aware you become, the more your vision grows with you in depth and complexity until your awareness and higher vibration permits you to see it in its entirety. It is in this way that you discover the Creator.

Here is a guided meditation that we have used at vision quests and Medicine Wheel gatherings throughout the United States and Canada. It is one that we have found very effective for leading groups into a simulated vision quest experience. It is one that you can use by prerecording your voice and becoming your own guide through the experience. Or you may read it aloud to a trusted friend or loved one, and then have that same individual read it for you and lead you through the experience.

Enter a state of a very relaxed frame of mind. When you have reached a deep level, when you have gone deep, deep, within – moving toward the very center of your essence – begin to tell yourself that you have the ability to visualize in your mind the conditions of your vision quest.

Tell yourself that you have the ability to tap into the eternal transmission of universal truth from which you may draw power and strength. You have the ability to evolve as a spiritual being.

Visualize yourself as a native American man or woman on a vision quest. Focus your thoughts on your performance of some mundane, monotonous physical task.

Perhaps like so many young native American men and women on a vision quest, you have found a small clearing in the forest which has a number of rocks of various sizes at one end of the nearly barren area. Pick up one of the rocks and carry it to the opposite side of the clearing. In your mind, see yourself carrying the rock. See yourself placing the rock down on the ground and turning around to get another rock. See yourself picking up a new rock, carrying it slowly to the other side of the clearing, and then another rock, and another, back and forth. Back and forth, over and over again.

Know and understand that you are performing this task for the sole purpose of depleting the physical self with monotonous exercise. Know and understand that you are distracting the unconscious mind with dull activity, that you are doing this to free the essential self within you, so that it can soar free of the physical body.

Feel now your body becoming very, very tired. Your body is feeling very heavy. It feels very, very dull.

You have no aching muscles or sore tendons, but you are very, very tired. Your physical body is exhausted. See yourself lying down on the blanket to rest, to relax.

Slowly you become aware of a presence. Someone has approached you and has come to stand next to you. As you look up at the figure, you see that it is a most impressive individual. It is a man who is looking at you with warmth and compassion.

The group pauses for a moment of instruction before going on to one of the high energy vortex sites during one of Brad and Sherry Steiger's NATIVE AMERICAN MEDICINE AND PROPHECY weekends in Sedona, Arizona.

And now you notice that he has been joined by a woman who is equally impressive, almost majestic in appearance.

Before you can open your mouth to speak, the man and the woman fade from your sight. They simply disappear. You realize that they were spirits, that they came to you from the spirit world to demonstrate to you that, in many ways, on many levels, you have a subtle, yet intense, partnership with the world of spirits. The spirit man and spirit woman have given you a visual sign of the reality of this oneness with all spiritual forms of life.

You have but a moment to ponder the significance of the spirit visitation when you become aware of a globe of bluish white light moving toward you. You are not afraid, for you sense a great spiritual presence approaching you.

As you watch in great expectation, the bluish white light begins to assume human form. As the light swirls and becomes solid, you behold before you a man or a woman whom you regard as a holy person, a saint, a master, an illumined one. The figure, so beloved to you, gestures to your left side. As you turn, you are astonished to see a marvelous link-up with other holy figures from all times, from all places, from all cultures. You see that these personages form a beautiful spiritual chain from prehistory to the present – and without doubt, the future.

The Holy One smiles benevolently, then bends over you and touches your shoulder gently. The Holy One's forefinger lightly touches your eyes, your ears, then your mouth. You know within that this act of touching symbolizes that you are about to see and to hear a wondrous revelation, which you must share with others.

Now, in a great rush of color and light, you are finding yourself elevated in spirit. You know that you have risen to a higher vibrational level. You have moved to a dimension where nonlinear, cyclical time flows around you.

From your previous limited perspective of Earth time, linear time, you are aware that you now exist in a timeless realm in eternal now. Stretching before you is something that appears to be a gigantic tapestry, a tapestry that has been woven of multi-colored living lights, lights that are pulsating, throbbing with life.

The energy of the Great Spirit touches your inner knowing, and you are made aware that you are becoming one with the great pattern of all life. In a marvelous, pulsating movement of beautiful lights and living energy, your soul feels a unity with all living things.

You see before you now an animal, any animal.

You become one with its essence. You become one with this level of awareness. Be that animal. Be that level of energy expression.

See before you a bird, any bird.

Now become one with its essence. Become one with its level of awareness. Be that bird. Be that level of energy expression.

See before you a creature of the waters, any creature.

Become one with its essence. Become one with its level of awareness. Be that marine creature. Be that level of energy expression.

See before you an insect – any insect crawling or flying.

Become one with its essence. Become one with its level of awareness. Be that insect. Be that level of energy expression.

See before you a plant – any flower, tree, grass, or shrub.

Become one with its essence. Become one with its level of awareness. Be that plant. Be that level of energy expression.

Know now that you are one with the unity of all plant and animal essence.

Know now that you forever bear responsibility to all plant and animal life.

You are one with all things that walk on two legs or four, with all things that fly, with all things that crawl, with all things that grow in the soil, or sustain themselves in the waters.

Listen carefully as your Spirit Guardian begins to tell you your secret name, your spirit name, the name that only you will know, that only you and your Guardian will share. It is the name by which your Guardian will contact you. Hear that name now.

And now you are being shown the image of an animal, a plant, a bird, a water creature, an image of one of the little brother or sisters other than humankind.

Focus upon that creature. See its beauty. Become one with its beauty. Know that this animal, this creature, is now your totem – that symbol which will come to you often in dreams and represent the spirit of yourself on another level of reality.

See before you another person, a man, a woman, young or old.

Go into that person. Become one with that person's essence. Become one with that person's level of awareness. Be that person. Be that level of energy expression.

Know now that it is never yours to judge another expression of humankind.

Know now that you have a common brotherhood and sisterhood with all of humankind.

Remember always that you must do unto your brothers and sisters as you would have them do to you. Remember always that the great error is to in any way prevent another's spiritual evolution.

At this eternal second in the energy of the Eternal Now, at this vibrational level of oneness with all living things, at this frequency of awareness of unity with the cosmos, your Spirit Guardian is permitting you to receive a great teaching vision of something about which you need to know for your good and your gaining.

Receive this great vision now. [Allow two minutes of silence.]

You will awaken at the count of five, filled with memories of your great vision quest.

When you awaken, you will feel morally elevated; you will feel intellectually illuminated. You will know that your spiritual essence is immortal. You will no longer fear death. You will no longer experience guilt or a sense of sin. You will feel filled with great charm and personal magnetism. You will feel better and healthier than ever before in your life, and you will feel a great sense of unity with all living things.

One, two, three, four, five, awake!

Chapter Three

FIRE: THE LINK BETWEEN THE NATURAL AND THE SUPERNATURAL WORLDS

Because of its integral role in the survival of the human species, fire has had aspects of religious significance to all peoples of the Earth.

Throughout the Old Testament, fire is emblematic of the Divine Presence.

So holy was the sacred fire in Rome that it was believed to represent the godhead; and if it should be extinguished, it could only be rekindled by the rays of the Sun.

In China, fire was extensively and prominently employed as a sacred medium, existing between the Ultimate Cause and humanity.

The Parasees of India worshipped the four elements, but gave prominence to fire.

The Hindus envision fire to be presided over by a subordinate spirit named Agni.

The American Indian tribes considered fire a link between the natural and the supernatural worlds. Fire constituted a mysterious "in-between realm" in which spirits were able to dwell.

The Cherokee believed that fire was an intermediate spirit between the Earth and the Sun.

Shawnee Medicine priests taught that the life within one's fleshly body and the fire in the hearth were one and the same thing and that both emanated from the same source – the Great Mystery.

In some tribes, a newborn child was waved over a fire in order to insure the guardianship of the spirit of the flames. In other tribal cultures, hunters held their moccasins above campfires as a ritual of protection against the bite of poisonous snakes.

AN ACTIVE AND INTELLIGENT BEING

Indian myths speak of fire as an active and intelligent being. In some tribal beliefs, the priests spoke of fire as having been born or brought with humankind from the supernatural world. Other tribal traditions tell that Medicine priests had to send for fire from the Man of Fire who lived across the immense waters. A spider was commissioned to answer their entreaties, and it returned with the mystic fire ensnared in its web.

As an intelligent being, fire was believed to be endowed with the faculty of sight. The Menominee tribes called comets, "The Seeing Fire in the Sky."

In the forest tribes, a tree that had been struck by lightning was carefully avoided. No human hand was to touch its broken branches. No part of the tree was allowed to be cut for fear of wounding the indwelling spirit of fire.

AN EMBLEM OF PURITY

The fire Power Symbol was used in sacrificial feasts as an emblem of purity. In certain rituals, fire was obtained directly from the heat of the Sun.

In the majority of religious rites, the fire was generally obtained by striking flint against flint. The wings of a white bird would be used to fan the sacred fire, for the breath was thought to be too impure on such occasions.

SACRED FIRES FOR SPECIAL FEASTS

The Creek tribes had a structure built in the form of a rotunda, within which were three circular divisions. The inner circle sheltered a fire that was constantly kept burning by Medicine priests. This fire was newly kindled on the occasion of the Feast of First Fruits. None but priests could attend or renew the fire.

Among Eastern tribes, the Feast of Fire was considered a ceremony of worship central to the most vital beliefs of the people. Fire was thought to be the heart of being. Upon its warmth depended all existence, both corporeal and spiritual.

The breath of life was identical to fire. Fire was alive.

It breathed and ate.

A Medicine priest kindled the flame upon the sacred hearth to begin the Feast of Fire, and it was a priest who formed the procession for the dance, whose participants would be exclusively limited to matrons, Medicine priests, and tribal chiefs who had distinguished themselves in service to their people.

One old account declares that the following hymn was sung during such a ritual:

> Great Spirit! Master of our lives! Great Spirit! Master of things visible and invisible, and who daily makes them visible and invisible. Great Spirit! Master of every other spirit, good or bad; command the good to be favorable unto us, and deter the bad from the commission of evil.
>
> O Grand Spirit! Preserve the strength and courage of our warriors, and augment their numbers, that they may resist oppression from our enemies, and recover our country and the rights of our fathers.
>
> O Grand Spirit! Preserve the lives of such of our old men as are inclined to give counsel to the young. Preserve our children and multiply their number, and let them be the comfort and support of declining age. Preserve our corn and our animals, and let no famine desolate the land. Protect our villages, guard our lives!
>
> O Great Spirit! When hidden in the west protect us from our enemies, who violate the night and do evil when thou art not present. Good Spirit! make known to us your pleasure by sending to us the Spirit of Dreams. Let the Spirit of Dreams proclaim thy will in the night, and we will perform it in the day; and if it say the time of some be closed, send them, Master of Life, to the great country of souls, where they may meet their friends, and where thou art pleased to shine upon them with a bright, warm, and perpetual blaze!
>
> O Grand, O Great Spirit! Hearken to the voice of the nations, hearken to all thy children, and remember us always, for we are descended from thee.

Immediately after this hymn, four quadrants formed one immense circle and danced and sang hymns descriptive of the power of Fire and of the Sun until nearly ten o'clock. The tribespeople then refreshed themselves in the village and camp, but assembled precisely at the hour of twelve. Then, forming a number of circles, commenced the adoration of the meridian sun. The following is said to be the literal translation of the midday address:

> Courage, nations, courage! The Great Spirit, now above our heads, will make us vanquish our enemies; he will cover our fields with corn, and increase the animals of our woods. He will see that the old be made happy, and that the young augment. He will make the nations prosper, make them rejoice, and make them put up their voice to him, while he rises and sets in their land, and while his heat and light can thus gloriously shine out.

The evening hymn, at the setting of the sun, was chanted in these words, after the people had formed into the segment of a circle:

> The nations must prosper; they have been looked upon by the Great Spirit. What more can they wish? Is not that happiness enough? See, he retires, great and content, after having visited his children with light and universal good.
>
> O Grand Spirit! sleep not long in the gloomy west, but return and call your people to light and life – to light and life – to light and life.

THE LOVING WARMTH OF THE SUN

According to Twylah Nitsch, the Sun was a symbol of love to the early Senecas.

The circle, the shape of the Sun, took on an added significance; it was symbolic of perfection and equality. The Sun's color was the most revered because of its beauty and magnificence. The Indians found themselves smiling whenever the Sun shone upon them. They believed that the Sun smiled at them all the time.

Smiling at someone and placing one's hand in another's signified the presence of love. To smile at someone was to convey a spiritual message of good will. Words were not always necessary where faith and love were present. The feelings that accompany love speak for themselves.

The Senecas held a fixed purpose in life, and that was to learn about the Great Mystery.

The Great Spirit – the Divine Supreme, Maker of All Things, Now and Forever.

The Great Spirit – the Eternal Mind, whose thoughts flow everlastingly.

The Great Spirit – the Master Designer, the Arranger of Patterns of All and Everything.

The Great Spirit – the Celestial Law, the Perpetuator of Perfection.

The Great Spirit – the Ethereal Voice. The Composer of the Harmony in Nature.

The Great Spirit – the Great Mystery, God.

THE DIVINE FIRE
AND THE GREAT MYSTERY

The Great Mystery, All-that-Is (God, if you prefer) is Divine Love. The essence of Divine Love is life.

The Sun is emblematic of the Living God that sustains all life through its warmth. The fire\sun symbol signifies the Divine Fire of All-That-Is, and the process of purification that enables one to become one with the Great Mystery.

Among the ancient writings of the Brahmins is the following passage:

"Truth constantly reveals itself by its own inward light, and the Divine Fire continually burning in the soul is sufficient worship."

SEEKING THE DIVINE FIRE WITHIN

Prophets of all belief constructs have often spoken of a "burning fire" within them that demands that they proclaim their revelations. Have you ever felt such a "Fire" within you?

Have you ever felt an urgency to reveal concepts or ideas that have come to you in dreams, visions, or meditation?

What is it from your dreams, visions, or meditation that you would most like to share with your family members? _____
_____

What aspects of a vision, dream or meditation would you most like to share with your friends? _____
_____

What "revelation" would you most like to share with the world?
_____

There are many common expressions that have entered our speech patterns which betray the universal acceptance of the fire symbol in our psyches. For example, "He's on fire with his ideas." "He's burning with desire for his sweetheart." How many other expressions of like manner can you list? _____

THE GIFT OF FIRE

Have you ever been lost for a time in a snowstorm or in a forest on a very cold night?

Memories of terrible vulnerability to hostile elements assist one in truly appreciating the gift of fire.

As an exercise, remember a time when you were very, very cold. Recall how you felt when you were finally brought into a warm place. Go back into those feelings, those memories, and relive your emotions.

Remember how your skin felt. . .how your nostrils tingled. . .how your arms may have stung or burned. Be aware of your senses of touch, smell. . .taste.

When you have become totally immersed in such a memory, sit quietly for a few minutes, then write down your special prayer of thanks to the Great Mystery, to the Living God, for the gift of fire.

MY SPECIAL PRAYER OF THANKS FOR THE GIFT OF FIRE

_____

_____

_____

_____

_____

_____

_____

_____

_____

POSITIVE AND NEGATIVE FIRE EXPERIENCES

What was the most positive experience that you have ever had around a fire {Fireplace, campfire, bonfire, etc.}? _____

Describe the most negative experience that you have ever had in association with fire: _____

How do you usually respond near a large, open fire? Are your feelings basically positive or negative? _____

Recall the single experience that you believe most formed your basic attitude toward fire. _____

Describe briefly any dreams that you might have had in which fire played a significant role. _____

THE FIRE OF INTENSE SPIRITUAL EXPERIENCE

Have you ever awakened at night and perceived what appeared to be an entity, glowing or luminous, that stood near your bed? _____

Have you ever had an intense religious or spiritual experience in which you felt that you were bathed in a brilliant fire or light? _____

THE DUAL NATURE OF FIRE

Fire is the sustenance of life. Fire is the symbol of the Divine.

There is, of course, the other side: Fire consumes; fire destroys. Fire lays waste to great forests and large cities.

Like all great energy forces, fire has a duality.

Religionists speak of a "Hell fire" that blazes forever.

And there are fires of suffering that burn away the dross and makes the spiritual warrior stronger.

Although the dualities of fire may seem worlds apart, the opposite ends, like most extremes, meet in a narrow line of balance. In all cases, fire purifies.

FIRE AS A MEDIUM FOR REVELATION AND INSPIRATION

The symbol for the Holy Spirit is most often a tongue of flame. God spoke to Moses from the burning bush.

Considering the agency of fire as a medium for revelation and inspiration, light a candle and assume a comfortable position so that you may safely focus your attention on its flame. You might see fit to play some appropriate background music, something inspirational, without lyrics to distract you.

Take a comfortably deep breath and exhale slowly. Repeat this process four times.

Sit in silence for several minutes and permit yourself to become receptive to any creative thoughts that may enter your consciousness. List them below so that you may have a record of your insights and inspirations: _____

_____

_____

FOCUSING THE DIVINE FIRE

Take a crystal in each hand and gently place them against your temples. Close your eyes and take three comfortably deep breaths.

Lower the crystals and hold them a few inches away from your Heart Chakra. Now breathe your intention to achieve an illumination experience into the crystals. Repeat the process three times.

Set the crystals before you. See that their tips are lightly touching.

Take three comfortably deep breaths and lower your head toward the larger of the crystals. *Imagine yourself being drawn into the larger crystal.* Visualize that your own energy is blending with the electromagnetic impulses of the crystal and that you are being pulled into the crystal.

Visualize yourself becoming one with the crystal energy for at least three minutes before you have a friend read the following process aloud to you. You may record your own voice to serve as your guide. It is also suggested that some appropriate inspirational music provide background score to heighten the effect.

Permit yourself to relax. . .totally and completely.

You will now invite the DIVINE FIRE to enter your psyche and enable you to become an instrument of balance, love, peace, strength, and inspiration.

You know that you have within you the ability to receive a spark of the DIVINE FIRE.

You know that you have the ability to be elevated to higher realms of consciousness and spiritual communion.

You know that you have the ability to become one with THE

SOURCE OF ALL THAT IS.

You know that you have the ability to tap into the eternal transmission of Universal Truths from which you may draw power and strength.

You know that you have the ability to evolve as a spiritual being.

You know that you have the ability to progress out of your old, physical limitations and to rise to a higher realm.

Visualize yourself now as the kind of spiritual seeker with whom you most identify. You have this ability.

You have the ability to see yourself as a MONK of the European, Mid-Eastern, Indian, or Oriental traditions.

You have the ability to see yourself as a NUN, PRIESTESS, ORACLE, or COSMIC CHANNEL.

You have the ability to see yourself as a disciplined traditional AMERICAN INDIAN on a Vision Quest.

Slowly, you become aware of a presence. Someone has approached you and has come to stand next to you. Wherever you see yourself now – a forest clearing, a temple garden, a high mountain plateau – you are aware that *someone* stands near you as you rest.

As you look up at the figure, you see that it is a most impressive individual. It is a man who is looking at you with warmth and compassionate interest.

And now you notice that he has been joined by a woman who is equally impressive, almost majestic in appearance. She smiles at you, and you feel somehow as if she stands before you enveloped in the mother vibration.

Before you can open your mouth to speak, the man and the woman fade from your sight. They simply disappear.

And now you realize that they came to you from the spirit world to demonstrate to you that, in many ways, on many levels, you have a subtle, yet intense, partnership with the world of spirits. The spirit man and spirit woman have given you a visual sign of the reality of this Oneness with all *spiritual* forms of life.

You have but a moment to ponder the significance of the spirit visitation when you become aware of two globes of bluish-white light moving toward you. You are not afraid, for you sense a great spiritual presence approaching you.

As you watch in reverential expectation, the first globe of bluish-white light begins to assume a human form. As the light swirls and becomes solid, you behold before you a man or a woman whom you regard as a Holy Person, a saint, a master, an illumined One.

This figure, so beloved to you, gestures to your left side. As you turn, you are astonished to see a marvelous linkup of other Holy Figures, from all times, from all places, from all cultures. You see that these personages form a beautiful spiritual chain, from prehistory to the present, and, without doubt, the future.

The Holy One smiles benevolently, then bends over you and touches your shoulder, Then, gently, the Holy One's forefinger lightly touches your eyes, then your ears, then your mouth. You know that this act of touching symbolizes that you are about to see and to hear a wondrous revelation, which, consequently, you must share with others.

As the Holy Figure begins to fade from your perception, the second globe of bluish-white light begins to materialize into human form.

The entity that forms before you now may be very familiar to you. You may very likely have seen this entity in your dreams. You may even have seen this entity materialize before you on previous occasions.

You may have been aware of this entity since your earliest memories, for standing before you now is your guide.

See the love in those eyes. *Feel* the love emanating toward you from your guide. This is one who has *always* loved you – just as you are. This is one who has always totally accepted you just as you are. This is one, who, with unconditional love, is concerned completely with your spiritual evolution. You feel totally relaxed, at peace, at One with your guide. And you feel totally loved.

Your guide's mouth is opening. *Listen.* Listen to the sound that issues forth. You hear it clearly and you understand it.

It may be a personal sound – a mantra. It may be a series of notes and words – your own personal song of attunement. It may be your guide's name.

Whatever the sound is, you hear it clearly and distinctly. And you have the inner awareness that whenever you repeat this sound – this mantra, this song, this name – you will be able to achieve instant At-Oneness with your guide.

Your guide is now showing you something for you to see. It is an object which you can clearly identify which will serve as a symbol to you in your dreams. It will serve as a symbol that you are about to receive a meaningful and important teaching in your dreams. Whenever you see this symbol in your dreams, you will understand that an important and significant teaching will follow.

That symbol fades from your sight, but you *will* remember it.

You are fascinated by what your guide now holds before you.

In your guide's hands is a tiny flame, a flame such as one might see on a match or a candle.

The flame flickers and dances. You cannot take your eyes from it. The flame seems to capture all of your attention and to pull you toward it. It is as if your very spirit is being pulled from your body and drawn toward the flame.

The flame is becoming brighter – brighter and larger. You cannot take your eyes from this strange, compelling flame. You can no longer see your guide. You can see only the flame. You are no longer aware of anything other than the flame. It is growing larger, larger and brighter, brighter and larger. It is as if there is nothing else in the entire universe but the flame – the flame and *you*.

You know now that this is the Divine Fire. You know now that this flame has appeared to bring you illumination. You know that it is not really a fire, not really a flame, but a divine and holy energy, the same energy that is interwoven with all of life, the same energy that interacts with all of life.

This energy now swirls around you, lightly tingling the body whenever it touches you. It is not at all an unpleasant sensation. It is, in fact, soothing yet strangely exhilarating at the same time.

The energy now caresses your body, gently, lovingly. You are aware of your body becoming cleansed, purified, healed of any ills, pains, and tension.

You know that from this moment onward, your physical health is going to be superb, better than it has ever been. You know that from this moment on, your physical energy is going to be increased. You know that your friends and your family will be commenting about your golden glow of health and vitality.

The energy of the Divine Fire now enters your body. It is now becoming One with you. It is becoming one with your cleansed and purified body. It is becoming one with your expectant spirit.

In a great rush of color and light, you now find yourself elevated in spirit. You have moved to a dimension where non-linear time, cyclical time, flows around you. From your previous limited perspective of Earth-time, linear time, you are aware that you now exist in a Timeless Realm, an Eternal Now.

At this eternal second in the energy of the Eternal Now, at this vibrational level of Oneness with all living things, at this frequency of awareness of unity with the Cosmos, the Divine Fire is permitting *you* to receive a great teaching vision of something about which you need to know for your good and your gaining. Receive this great vision – *now*! [Allow at least a one minute pause.]

You will awaken at the count of five, filled with memories of your great vision. When you awaken you will feel morally elevated; you will feel intellectually illuminated; you will know that your essence is immortal; you will no longer fear death; you will see clearly all lessons you need to learn from past mistakes or errors. You see and feel them completely. Now see any remaining fear or guilt you may still harbor. Now let it all go. . .like a helium-filled balloon, let it go. You will no longer experience guilt or a sense of sin; you will feel filled with a great charm and personal magnetism; you will feel better and healthier than ever before in your life; you will feel a great sense of unity with *all* living things.

One. . .two. . .three. . .four. . .five. . .awaken!

Chapter Four

SPIRIT MESSENGERS
AND GUARDIANS

Among all living beings there are few that inspire more worshipful thoughts than the winged ones of the air. It has been observed that the flight of a bird arouses a mysterious instinct within the human soul. Some people have found their eyes dilating, their hearts beating more rapidly, their bodies vibrating with emotion as they watched a bird soaring into limitless space. And it seems that it was this very soul-stirring energy that caused the ancient people to recognize the power of the winged ones in sculpture, painting, myth, and legend.

As we stood in the Inca's Temple of the Sun in Cusco, Peru, we heard of the hummingbirds that adorned the ornaments of godlike, majestic figures as representative of the elder world. Perhaps it seemed to the ancient Incas that the tiny bird's blurred wings in their furious motion were a suitable emblem of the unseen transition of the human soul.

The Chippewas had a tradition that in the time-before-time there existed a bird of supreme majesty that descended to Earth, which was then only a vast globe of water. The bird's eyes were fire; its glance was lightning, and the motion of its wings rippled the air with thunder. When its talons touched the water, the Earth Mother arose from the deep, bringing with her all manner of animals.

Many other tribes have traditions that tell of birds as agents of creation, and the winged ones became objects of religious ceremony among many of the native peoples. The journal of an early Roman Catholic priest records that the first time the Amerindian members of the California mission saw the representation of a dove over the altar, they asked if it was the Christian's thunderbird.

Although the Holy Spirit is commonly portrayed as a descending dove, the eagle has also been used to depict the swift and mighty power of God. Hebrew tradition also utilizes the eagle, together with the bull and the lion, as emblems of the Divine Being.

Just before we lighted candles and formed a circle of light in an especially sacred site within the ancient Peruvian city of Machu Picchu, we offered our blessings as Children of the Eagle {the United States} to the Children of the Condor {the Incas and their descendants among the contemporary Peruvians}. Receiving our goodwill was an able young shaman's apprentice named Rainbow who had told us earlier that the presence of the great condor soaring high above the tallest peaks in the Andes is an ever-present reminder that the Incas of old will one day return to Earth from their home in the stars.

In his work *The World's Rim,* Hartly Burr Alexander expresses his opinion that the Thunderbird may be taken as a symbol of a second great North American culture group that issued from the North and the East and impinged upon the plateau cultures of the Southwest. For it is, Alexander rightly comments, in the forests and plains of the great continental river valleys that the "sky warriors," the Thunderers, are most often sighted and revered.

Kuichy, (which means rainbow) an apprentice Shaman and guide, and Sherry Steiger at a reverse energy vortex in Peru. This site is known for hundreds of mysterious accidents involving moving transportation such as planes, cars, trains, etc.

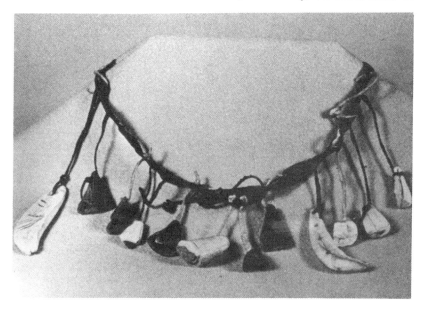

This Tlingit shaman's necklace of teeth, bones, and bear's claws was collected by G. Emmons in 1902. The Tlingits, a Northwest Coast ribe, celebrated their religious beliefs in the cedar, bone, and ivory readily available to them.

As Alexander phrases it, the Thunderers are represented "... as great birds of the hawk family: their eyes and beaks send forth the arrowy lightnings, their sweeping wings beat the air into thunders, their plumes are rain-dripping, and their flight is wind-swift. The warrior paints their emblem upon his person, his shield, his pony, his medicine, and the priest. . . .seeks the powerful protection of this chieftain of the skies." Cross-culturally, Alexander notes that the falcon of Egypt, the eagle of Assyria, Persia, and Rome, as well as the American bald eagle, ". . .are all emblematically akin to the Thunderbird."

An early European traveler among the Mandan Indians told of observing a religious ceremony that involved two white painted eagles that had been carved out of poplar wood. The images had their wings in an outstretched position and their bodies were raised five feet from the ground. On the inner side of each of the notched pieces of wood on which the eagles rested was the figure of a man with buffalo horns formed of white clay. The images of the eagles, together with a painted figure of a panther, were said to represent powerful supernatural mysteries, and the visitor stated that the presiding Medicine Priest offered sacrificial reverence to the forms.

In the sacred works of the Hindu, we learn of the great Garuda, a large, eagle-like bird, that is often spoken of as a companion to Lord Vishnu. In some representations, Vishnu is depicted as riding on the back of this giant winged one.

The Scandinavians revered a great eagle which dwelt upon the branches of the tree Yggdrasil, a symbol of universal nature. In many instances, the old Medicine Priests attached the plumage and the heads of hawks to their shoulders, turning the beaks inward as if in communication with them. Similar depictions of the heads of hawks may be seen in certain pictures of the Norse god Odin.

Among some tribes there was a tradition of placing three long tail feathers from a hawk on each side of a Medicine Priest who claimed prophetic abilities. If the priest was too often in error or was considered of a negative disposition, he was allowed to wear only three feathers on only one side of his head, thus becoming known as a "One-sided Priest."

Among the Iowa tribe, there was a species of hawk that was considered to be so sacred that it was killed only to obtain select portions of its body for the most powerful of medicines. This particular hawk was thought to inhabit only the highest cliffs of the most intimidating mountains and could only be obtained with the utmost difficulty. The Iowas also believed that the hawk had the supernatural faculty of remaining for a long time on the wing. Those who stalked the winged one and were unsuccessful in bringing back its sacred body for medicine stated that they had seen the hawk fly away toward the Land of the Blessed.

CHANT OF THE SACRED HAWK

The hawks turn their heads nimbly 'round;
They turn to look back on their flight.
The spirits of *Gee-zhi-gong* [the sun place] have
whispered them words;
They fly with their messages swift.
They look as they fearlessly go;
They look to the very ends of the world.
Their eyes catch the light, and their beaks
can deliver harm.

Some students of the Amerindian tradition have remarked that the above chant reveals a mythological notion that the ancient Medicine Priests believed the birds to be intimately acquainted with humankind's destiny. As in so many other cultures, the traditional priests seem to have held

Ancient attire and sacred
medicine bag of a Native
Peruvian shaman, preserved
in a museum in Cusco, Peru.

birds – particularly hawks, ravens, and falcons – to be harbingers of
good or evil. The winged ones, after all, live in the open air, rising
through the very atmosphere wherein resides the essence of the Sky
Father, the Great Mystery. It would behoove the Medicine Priest to seek
diligently to interpret the messages relayed by the winged ones.

Some tribes maintained that even more than bearing omens, certain
birds might actually be spirit beings who had clothed themselves in the
winged ones' forms. If a bird seemed to be flying with unusual rapidity
of flight, a Medicine Priest might suspect a supernatural purpose.

MEETING THE SPIRIT GUARDIAN DURING THE VISION QUEST

Some years ago, a dear friend named Clark described how he had received his spirit guardian during a vision quest conducted by the Winnebago tribe in Wisconsin.

> I wouldn't have been quite thirteen. We were given pre-
> liminary tutoring for several weeks on what to expect and
> what was expected of us. Then we were asked to go out into
> the woods and pick a spot where there was a stream. We were
> told that we must not bring food or seek out berries or any
> kind of food. We were also told that we must not seek shelter,
> but must remain exposed to the elements, to the rain or to the
> sun. We were to weaken our bodies and to continue praying at

least three times a day for our guide.

. . .We prayed to Manitou, the Supreme Being.

The main thought behind the rite is to completely exhaust the body as quickly as possible. One of the exercises the Winnebagos suggested was to find a place where there were rocks, so that we might pick them up and run with them from one place to another. Make a pile one place, then pick them up and carry them back again, repeating the process again and again.

You see, this exercise enabled one to busy his conscious mind with a monotonous physical activity while the subconscious mind was concentrating on the attainment of one's guide.

After a while, one would begin to see wildlife that would seemingly become friendlier. After a time, some creature would approach, as if to offer itself as a totem, or guide. It could be a bird, a chipmunk, a gopher, a badger. If the boy were very hungry, and if he were afraid of staying out in the wilderness alone, he could accept the first creature that approached and say that he had found his guide. But we were taught that if we could endure, Manitou, or one of his representatives in human form, would appear and talk to us.

I spent twelve days fasting and awaiting my guide. I had many creatures, including a beautiful deer, come up to me and allow me to pet them. The deer, especially, wanted to stay. But I had been told that if I did not want to accept a form of life that offered itself to me, I should thank it for coming, tell it of its beauty, its strength, its intelligence, but tell it also that I was seeking one greater.

On the twelfth day, an illuminated form appeared before me. Although it seemed composed primarily of light, it did have features and was clothed in a long robe.

"You I have waited for," I said. And it replied: "You have sought me, and you I have sought."

Then it faded away. But it had appeared before me just as real as you are!

On the evening that each boy was required to appear before the Winnebago council to tell of his experience, my guide was accepted as genuine. And I don't think there is any way that any young boy could have fooled that tribal council. They knew when he had had a real experience and when he had used something as an excuse to get back to the reservation and get something to eat.

One thing that we were taught is that we must never call upon our guides until we had exhausted very bit of physical energy and mental resource possible. Then, after we had employed every last ounce of our own reserve, we might call upon our guide and it would appear.

THE CONCEPT OF GUARDIAN SPIRITS

The concept of ultra-physical beings – call them guardian spirits, angels, etheric masters, or what you will – materializing to assist humans in times of crisis appears to be universal.

These entities may be one of three things:

1.) Messenger entities with a more than casual interest in man, who come from the Great Spirit to perform precisely the functions which they claim.

2.) Externalized projections of man's own High Self (his Superconscious) which appear to help man help himself.

3.) A manifestation in which the Great Spirit reveals itself to the recipient in an appropriate form which will permit him to perceive the revelation in the manner most meaningful to him.

Clark has said that his guardian spirit has responded to his calls for help and that on two occasions it has appeared to warn him of approaching danger. Whether the ostensible spirit was an independent intelligent entity concerned about Clark's welfare or whether the manifestation was due to his superconscious level of mind receiving information through other than sensory means and externalizing the knowledge as a warning spirit, he did not hesitate to act upon the information received.

The traditional Amerindian treats his guardian spirit with respect, and he uses the information given to him in dreams and in visions as lessons about himself to be used in the most effective performance of his personal medicine.

VISUALIZING YOUR SPIRIT GUARDIAN

You should be seated comfortably in a place and at a time when you will not be disturbed for at least thirty minutes. Inspirational music playing in the background usually proves to be of great benefit in accelerating the awesome experience of encountering your loving, benevolent Spirit Guardian.

Your success in this very important exercise depends upon your desire to make contact with the multidimensional being that serves as your Spirit Guardian. **Be certain that you are in an extremely relaxed state before the voice of a friend – or your own prerecorded voice –**

leads you through the following process:

As your body lies now in a deep sleep, your mind, your Essential Self, is very much aware that you are being surrounded by a beautiful golden light, and you feel the warmth of the light from the source of All-That-Is beginning to stimulate your Crown Chakra.

You are becoming one with the feeling of being loved unconditionally by an intelligence who has always loved you just as you are.

Now you are sensing the presence of an intelligence that you have always known on one level of consciousness. You have known that this intelligence has been near you ever since you were a child.

You are becoming aware of the sensation of warmth in both your Heart Chakra and your Crown Chakra. You are aware of a ray of light that is connecting your essence to the higher vibrations of this entity – this light being that is approaching you.

Now you are seeing that the golden light has acquired a tinge of pink. See it begin to swirl around you, moving faster and faster until it begins to acquire a form and substance. Now you see the shape of a body, of hair, of a beautiful smile and a loving face.

You are becoming especially aware of the eyes. You feel the love, the unconditional love, that flows out to you from those eyes. You feel yourself becoming even more enveloped in the warmth of unconditional love from this higher intelligence that is approaching.

You are aware in your inner self that, materializing before you now, is the image of your spiritual guide. You have an inner knowing that your guide has come to take you to a special place where you will be able to receive profound and meaningful visions designed to aid you to achieve your fullest good and your utmost potential.

Your guide stretches forth a firm, but loving, hand. Take that hand in your own.

Feel the love flowing through you. Feel the vibration of one who has always loved you. Feel the vibration of one who has come to take you to a special place where profound visions await you.

You see a purple mist clouding up around you as you begin to move through Time and Space with your spiritual guardian.

Now you are seeing yourself in a holy place.

You may be seeing yourself in a beautiful garden that lies before a majestic temple.

You may be seeing yourself in a sacred place in a forest.

You may be seeing yourself high on some mountain retreat.

You may be remembering a scene from a past life experience in which you devoted yourself to spiritual service. You may be remembering a life as a nun, a priest, a Medicine man or woman, a yogi, a high priestess.

Whatever you might have been, you remember this holy place that now appears before you.

There is now a vibration in the air as if bells are chiming. At that sound, at that signal, a wise spirit teacher comes to meet you.

See the love in those eyes as the teacher sees you. Look deeply into the eyes of that beloved teacher. As you do so you will learn the name of this great master teacher.

Become totally aware of your spiritual teacher. See his clothes, his body, his face, his eyes, his mouth, the way he holds his hands.

The teacher tells you that he has a gift of greeting for you. He says it is a very special gift that will aid you in achieving a deep and powerful vision.

He reaches within his robe and brings forth a leather bag. He opens the leather bag and hands you the gift.

You look at the gift. See what it is. Take the gift. Feel it. Know it. Tell the teacher how you feel about him and his gift.

Now you are once again aware that your spiritual guide is beside you. Your guide has taken your hand to walk beside you and the master teacher.

The three of you are now walking in a tunnel. The master teacher is leading you to a secret place.

As you walk, you turn to your spiritual guide and you say, "Oh, guide, one who has loved me and cared for me since before my awareness, please tell me what your name is."

If it is to be at this time, your guide will reveal the name by which you might summon his vibration again – the name by which you might call upon this source of strength. [Pause 30 seconds for the reception of the name.]

Experience your emotions as you walk between your guide and your master teacher. Feel deeply your expectations.

See the torches set into the walls. Be aware of any aromas, any sounds, any sights.

You are now in a great cave. Look around you slowly. See statues and paintings arranged around the room. See them and remember them.

Your spiritual teacher is now showing you a great crystal that is supported on a golden tripod. As you lean forward to stare into the crystal, your spiritual teacher tells you that he will now permit you to see a meaningful vision.

He tells you that you will now see all that you need to see at this time. You will see all that is necessary for your present level of under-standing. You will see a vision that will be completely individualized for you and for your particular needs.

See that vision now!

[Allow at least two minutes for the vision to manifest.]

You are coming awake. The purple mist of time is leaving you.

You are coming awake with remembrance of all you need to know for your good and your gaining.

You are feeling wonderful both in body and in mind. You are coming awake filled with love and filled with full remembrance of all you need to remember for your good and your gaining. Awaken!

THE BENEFITS OF REGULAR MEDITATION

The benefits obtained from regular periods of meditation are numerous. Meditation offers you peace, inner balance, and an unruffled attitude toward all that comes your way. All of these benefits are valuable to the practicing Medicine Person. They give a solid foundation from which to sally forth into the unknown. They also provide an ethical basis from which to determine the proper uses of mental powers.

With the continued practice of meditation you will learn to sharpen and to discipline those two necessary factors, mind and will. And, with strengthened mind and a directed will, the powers of Medicine will be more readily yours.

Set aside a certain time of the day – preferably the same time every day – and declare it to be your meditation period.

If you adhere to your schedule, and, say you choose eleven o'clock in the morning, you will soon find that you subconsciously prepare for this hour. You may be engaged with some business at your office or finishing up the morning breakfast dishes, and an inner alarm will go off, telling you it is your meditation time. Also, when you become truly adept at achieving a meditational high, it will not be uncommon for you to experience a kind of "rush" at the appointed hour.

Once you have chosen a time period, settle yourself in a comfortable position, either sitting upright or lying down. The back must be straight. Make sure you sit in a position that can be maintained without some part of your body falling asleep. If you prefer to lie down, try the floor. The floor will keep your back straighter and be a better guard against falling asleep.

Your upright position may be either cross-legged, Indian yoga style, Egyptian yoga style [sitting in a chair with legs uncrossed, feet flat on

Brad and Sherry Steiger at the ruins of the pre-Inca Indians in Machupiccu, Peru. This breathtaking and extensive site is still being excavated.

Ancient ceremonial dress of a Peruvian Inca Medicine man.

Kuichy and Brad Steiger. Kuichy told us that wisdom to the Indian is natural. He points out the definition of Indian is "close to nature."

---

the floor, hands resting on your knees] or tailor fashion.

The most important thing is that you be comfortable, and that your back be straight. The position of the hands for meditation is not of paramount importance. The only thing to remember is to not clasp the hands on top of the head. This interrupts the flow of power.

Once you have settled comfortably you must relax completely and empty your mind of all thoughts. This can be extremely difficult to do, but continued practice will eventually bring you to a state of complete relaxation.

SONG OF THE SACRED WHITE BUFFALO WOMAN

I was here before the rains and the violent sea.
I was here before the snows and the hail.
I was here before the mountains and the winds.
I am the spirit of Nature.

I am in the light that fills the earth, and in the
darkness of nighttime.
I give color to nature, for I am in nature's growth
and fruits.
I am again in nature where themes of mystic wisdom
are found.
I am in your chants and laughters.
I am in the tears that flow from sorrow.
I am in the bright joyous eyes of the children.

I am in the substance that gives unity, completeness,
and oneness.
I am in the mountains as a conscious symbol to all man
kind when earth's face is being scarred with
spiritual undone.
I am in you when you walk the simple path of the redman.

I am in you when you show love of humankind, for I also
give love to those who are loving.
I am in the response of love among all humans, for this is
a path that will find the blessing and fulfillment of the
Great Spirit.

[Translated by Dallas Chief Eagle, Teton Sioux]

REMEMBERING A PAST LIFE AS A MEMBER OF AN AMERICAN INDIAN TRIBE

Whether or not one truly accepts the doctrine of reincarnation, many men and women who seek a deeper understanding of shamanism and Medicine Power have found it useful to visualize a life experience as the member of an American Indian tribe. Here is a technique that we have used with great effectiveness:

Begin to relax the body as a friend reads the following visualization aloud. Once again, if you prefer, you may record your own voice reading this process into a tape recorder so that it is your own vibration that will guide you through the relaxation and projection process. Ethereal music will be a great asset. Just be certain that your background music has no lyrics to distract you.

Permit yourself to relax completely. Use any of the techniques previously provided in this book or any other method that totally relaxes you.

The Real You within your physical body is becoming aware of a beautiful figure robed in white standing near your relaxed body.

This beautiful figure is surrounded by an aura, a halo of golden light, and you know at once that you are beholding a Spirit Guardian who has come to take the *Real You* out of your physical shell and to travel with you to a higher dimension where you will be able to receive knowledge of a past life as an American Indian that you need to know about.

This may be a past life in which you may see a good many men and women who are with you in your present life. You may, in that time, be working at a task left unfinished, learning a lesson left unaccomplished that you should complete in your present life experience.

Whatever you see, it will be for your good and your gaining; and your guide will be ever near, allowing nothing to harm you. Your guide will be ever ready to protect you.

Now you permit your guardian to take you by your hand and to lift the *Real You* out of your body.

Don't worry. Your spirit–the *Real You* – will always return to your body, but for now you are free to soar into the past, totally liberated of time and space.

A swirling purple mist is moving all around you; and hand in hand with your guardian, you begin to move higher and higher, higher and higher.

You seem to be floating through space, moving gently through space, moving through all of time.

Time itself seems to be like a spiral moving around you, a spiral never ending, never beginning, never ending, never beginning.

You know that you have the ability to move back through time and to see a past life as an American Indian that you need to know about for your soul's evolution; a past life that may tell you very much about your present life.

Ahead of you, suspended in space, is a great golden door. And you know that when you step through that door you will be able to explore an important past life as a member of an Indian tribe.

You will be able to see the reasons why your soul chose the parents, the brothers and sisters, the friends, the mate, the talents of that time.

You will see the soul-chosen purpose for the agonies, troubles, pains, and griefs of that life experience.

Now your guide is ushering you to the great golden door. The door is opening, and you step inside....

You see yourself as you were when you were a child in that life.

You see the color of your eyes, your hair, your skin. You see clearly what sex you are.

Now see your body unclothed. See if you have any scars, birthmarks, or other peculiar characteristics that are visible on your naked body.

Now you are clothed. See yourself in characteristic clothing for that time. Understand the name of the tribe into which you have been born.

A man and a woman are now approaching you. Look at their eyes. It is the man and woman who are your *father* and *mother* in *that* life.

Understand what kind of relationship you have with them. Do they love you? Understand you? Reject you?

And now, look at their eyes and see if either of them are with you in your present life experience and have rejoined you to complete work left unfinished. . .to master a lesson left unlearned.

Now, in that same past lifetime as an American Indian, scan the vibrations of any other relative and see if any other family member from that time is with you in your present life.

In that same lifetime you are growing older, moving into young adulthood, and you see yourself performing some *favorite activity*, a game, a sport, a hobby, that becomes so very much a part of your life.

You see yourself performing that activity, and you understand how it will become impressed on your present life pattern.

You are now beginning to see clearly and to understand what *work* you did in that life as an American Indian. . .how you provided for yourself or for others. . .how you will spend your days.

Someone is approaching you from that tribal situation. Look into the eyes.

This may be someone who is your chief, your overseer.

This may be someone who is your subordinate.

But this is someone with whom you interacted closely during your daily tasks.

For your good and your gaining, look at the eyes; see if this person is with you in your present-life experience and has rejoined you to complete work left undone, to learn a lesson left unaccomplished.

Now, in that same lifetime as an American Indian, you are seeing yourself in a scene in which you had to struggle against great odds in order to achieve a meaningful goal. Everything that you see will be for your good and your gaining. Nothing will disturb you. Nothing will distress you. You will be able to see everything from a detached and unemotional point of view.

You may be seeing yourself in a scene of strife; you may even be seeing yourself fighting in a war; but you are seeing the scene clearly. You are detached, unemotional.

You are now seeing a friend or a loved one who supported you throughout your great struggle. This is one who was always there, who never failed you.

Look deep into the loving eyes of that one who always loved and supported you. See if that friend, that loved one, came with you in your present life experience, to complete a lesson left unlearned, to finish work left undone. Look into the eyes, and you will know.

And now you are looking into the eyes of one who steadfastly opposed you in that lifetime. This is one who tried to block everything you attempted.

Look into those eyes, deep into those eyes, and see if that one who opposed you came with you in your present life experience, to complete a lesson left unlearned, to finish work left undone. Look into the eyes, and you will know.

And now, for your good and your gaining, see if you attained your goal!

As you move away from the situation of strife, you are beginning to feel the *vibrations of love* moving all around you. You are aware of someone standing there, to your left, standing there in the shadows.

You are feeling love – warm, peaceful sensations of love – moving all around you, as you realize that standing there in the shadows is the person whom you love most in that lifetime.

Look at the eyes. Feel the love flowing toward you from those beautiful eyes of your beloved.

Look at the smile of recognition on those lips as the beloved one sees you and begins to move toward you.

This is the one with whom you shared your most intimate moments – your hopes, your dreams, your moments of deepest love. And yes, your sorrows, your hurts, your moments of deepest pain.

This is the one who always cared, who always loved and supported you.

Go to these arms. Feel those beloved arms around you.

Now, for your good and your gaining, look at the eyes. See if this beloved one is with you in your present-life experience.

See if your love, like a golden cord, has stretched across time, space, generations, years, to reunite you in the same beautiful love vibrations.

See if you have come together again to work out a task left incomplete, a lesson left unlearned.

With a flash of insight your guide is showing *you why* you lived that life as an American Indian and why you lived it with those whom you did.

You see clearly *why you* had to come again to put on the fleshly clothes of Earth in your present life.

You see *why* certain people from that life are with you now, and why they have rejoined you to complete work left undone, to master a lesson left unlearned.

In another flash of insight you are seeing and understanding *why* you came to Earth for the very *first* time, centuries ago.

You are remembering *why* you chose to put on the Karmic vibrations of Earth and come to this planet for the very first time.

You are remembering clearly *why* you came here. You are remembering your true mission in life.

You see and understand clearly what you are to do in your present life that will most aid you to accomplish your mission.

You are filled with a wonderful sense of well-being for now you know what you must do. You see clearly what you *must* do to fulfill totally your true mission in life. You no longer feel sensations of frustration and anxiety.

Now you *know*. You know why you came to Earth, why you chose to put on the clothes of Earth, why you chose to assume the Karmic vibration of this planet.

You are beginning to awaken, feeling very, very good. . .

very, very positive.

You are filled with a beautiful, glowing sense of your mission.

You are filled with the positive knowledge that you will be able to accomplish so much more good and gaining toward your true mission now that you are filled with awareness of your future lifetime.

Now you understand so very much more of the great pattern of your total life experience.

And you know that your spirit guardian will aid you, will assist you in completing your life mission, in accomplishing what you truly came here to do.

Awaken with positive feelings of love, wisdom, and knowledge.

Awaken feeling very, very good in the body, mind, and spirit.

Awaken feeling better than you have felt in weeks, in months, in years. *Awaken* filled with love, filled with knowledge.

Chapter Five

TOUCH THE STAR PEOPLE

The Indians of old regarded the movements of the stars and planets as entities regulated by their own indwelling power. They believed the larger stars had been appointed by the Great Mystery as guardians of the smaller ones. Clusters of stars were thought to be villages of Light Beings, and the constellations were believed to be council-gatherings of spirit entities. The following tradition was told by one of the Iowa tribes:

> Many years ago a child, when very young, observed a star in the heavens that attracted him more than any other. As the child grew to manhood his attachment increased. His thoughts dwelt continually upon this Beauty of the night.
>
> One day while hunting, as he sat down travel-worn, and weary with his ill-success, his beloved star appeared to him and comforted him with encouraging words, and then conducted him to a place where he found a great plenty and variety of game. From this time the young man showed a wonderful improvement in the art of hunting, and soon became celebrated in this pursuit.

It is interesting to note the universality of the belief in the stars as the residences of spiritual beings who have a connection with, and a mysterious relationship to, human souls. In the Egypt of Ramses the Great, such a belief exercised a great influence over the cosmology of the people, who linked individual destinies to the motions of the stars. The priestcraft of that time prophesied the temperament, life, and death of newborn infants from the conjunction of the planets at the hour of birth. Some scholars suggest that the origin of astrology may be traced to this period of history.

The ancient Persians kissed their hands at the stars in reverence, picturing each of them being governed by presiding spirits. Six of these spirits were known as the Amshaspands, the Immortal Holy Ones, who were thought to be under the immediate rule of Ormuzd, the King of Light. The Immortal Holy Ones conveyed the prayers of inferior spirits and of humans to Ormuzd and served as models of purity and perfection to lesser beings.

The native peoples of New Zealand believe in star spirits, but they conceive of the entities as being human souls who once had mortal bodies and who once resided on the Earth Mother.

In the hieroglyphic writing of the ancient Egyptians it has been asserted that the symbol for "star" signified a guiding or ministering spirit, a belief that would have been very similar to that of the American Indian tribes, who felt specific guidance from Star Beings.

LEGEND OF THE MORNING STAR
[WABUN-AN-NUNG]

The following is a legend of "The young spirit that sits in the morning star."

> Two children, brother and sister spirit beings, after having lived together several years, were obliged to separate. The sister was to go to the Place of the Breaking Light – *Waubunong* – the brother, to the rocks and hills.
>
> When they were about to separate, the sister said: "When you look in the east and see beautiful red clouds floating along the sky, believe that I am painting and adorning myself." The brother replied: "I will dwell upon the rocks that look toward the east, that I may gaze upon thee and delight in thy beauty."
>
> A sound of many winds now came upon the ears of the two, and soon the four spirit-winds of the heavens came forth and lifted up the sister spirit being and wafted her into the Place of Light, where she was changed into the Morning Star. Her brother, being left on earth, became a *Puckwudjinie*, [wood spirit] and dwelt upon the hills and rocks that looked towards the east, where he could see in the morning the red clouds with which his sister adorned herself as she stood in her star-lodge in the sky.

The Chippewa relate a myth in which a disappointment in love has its compensation in the hero's metamorphosis into a firefly, which betook itself to the sky, where it became the Northern Star. They called this star *No-adj-man-guet*, the "man who walks behind the loon-bird."

THE WANDERING STAR

A quarrel arose among the stars, when one of them was driven from its home in the heavens, and descended to the earth. It wandered from one tribe to another, and it was seen hovering over the camp-fires when the people were preparing to sleep.

Among all the people in the world, only one could be found who was not afraid of this star, and this was a daughter of a Chippewa. She was not afraid of the star, but admired and loved it. When she awoke in the night she always beheld it, for the star loved the maiden.

In midsummer the young girl, on going into the woods for berries, lost her way, when a storm arose. Her cries for rescue were only answered by the frogs.

A lonely night came, and she looked for her star in vain. A storm overcast the sky, and at length caught her in its fury and bore her away.

Many seasons passed, during which the star was seen dimmed and wandering in the sky. At length, one autumn, it disappeared.

Then a hunter saw a small light hanging over the water within the marshlands in which he was hunting. He returned to announce the strange sight,

"That," said an old wise man, "was the star driven from heaven, now wandering in search of our lost maiden, our beautiful child of the Chippewas."

HYMN TO THE PLEIADES, THE STAR DANCERS

Their sparkling eyes and lightly dancing feet
spin the clouds and give life to the four winds.
Their song of love and beauty blends
with the medicine drums they beat.
Racing, circling, whirling, chasing. . .
now receding.
They dance until the night sky
becomes one with the dawn.

AMERICAN INDIANS AND
THE STAR PEOPLE

The last few years have brought us a plethora of books expounding the thesis that the gods of old were actually ancient astronauts encouraging our emergent civilization with spurts of technological knowledge from their extraterrestrial laboratories.

The same books that have put forward the ancient astronaut thesis have also boggled the contemporary brain with accounts suggestive of extraterrestrial intervention in Europe, South America, Asia, and Africa. North American "gods" have, by and large, been overlooked, but nearly all of the Amerindian tribes have a rich and varied tradition of an interaction with the "Sky People," or "Star People," that is as extensive as fairy lore is among the natives of the British Isles. Amerindians, for example, have been aware of "magic circles" left by the Star People, just as their British counterparts know of the "fairy rings," and the modern UFO investigator examines strange, scorched circles left in farmers' fields and meadows.

Interestingly, the guidelines for Amerindian-Star People interaction, which were no doubt derived over centuries of trial and error, bear amazing similarities to the observations compiled by British and European countryfolk regarding the woodland gentry. And just as there are legends in Great Britain and Europe which would suggest that, in certain instances, the melding between humankind and their other-worldly companions became extremely intimate, so are there Amerindians who believe that such a blending may have taken place between their own kind and those from the stars.

There are certain risks involved in ascribing "ancient astronaut" motifs to petroglyphs (stone carvings) and pictographs (stone paintings). These may have been inspired by an artistic flight of fancy rather than an alien spaceship. "Domed space helmets" often turn out to be representations of horned headdresses, exaggerated in size to denote a chief's prowess and acumen or a medicine man's power and skill. However, some petroglyphs and pictographs are worthy of examination as a record of Amerindian interaction with the "Star People."

Thirty miles northeast of Price, Utah, is the beginning of Nine Mile Canyon, one of the most unusual canyons in the United States. Prior to 1100 A.D., the Fremont culture occupied the canyon, and the records they left in the form of petroglyphs and pictographs comprise the heaviest concentration of rock art in the world today.

The Fremont people developed their own art style, which, interest-

Petroglyphs, Indian "rock writing," recounts many legendary events, such as the visitation of the "Star People."

ingly, was typified by horned, trapezoidal-bodied, human-like "anthropomorphs." Were these creatures somehow symbolic of nature spirits? Or did they truly represent visitations by beings decidedly different from the other Amerindian neighbors of the Fremont people?

In one dramatic petroglyph in Nine Mile Canyon, one may view an unusual depiction of one of these horned (an ancient astronaut enthusiast might say, "antenna-spouting") anthropomorphic figures. In this instance, the creature is standing before a row of upraised human hands, which seem to imply awe, reverence, or fear. To the anthropomorph's left, there is a disc-like object. To the disc's left, there is an upside-down anthropomorph faintly etched in the stone.

Another petroglyph in Nine Mile Canyon shows what is definitely a scorpion standing between two mysterious figures. Some authorities have said that the etchings represent a fish and a tree, perhaps worked in an experimental style by some venturesome Fremont artist. Others, though, have wondered if the petroglyph might not pay homage to a dramatic energy or power assigned to a strange-blob-like object that had the ability to "sting like a scorpion."

John Magor, writing in *Canadian UFO Report* describes a most intriguing "flying object" pictograph which is located in a natural grotto near Christina Lake, B.C. The drawing depicts a white disc with black wing-like protuberances, hovering over four figures who appear to have bent their knees in an attitude of reverence. Squiggly lines, perhaps suggestive of rays of light, emanate from the top of the object. Longer, more irregular lines, possibly portraying smoke or fire energy, extend from the bottom of the disc.

Magor points out that although it was a practice of these primitive artists to depict exactly what they saw, they were no doubt limited by their inability to draw in depth. In order to compensate for this lack of perception, the artist may have tilted the object to indicate its discoid appearance. At the same time, he probably retained the wing-like rim outline, which no doubt impressed him.

Despite the limitations of paint upon rock, Magor feels that the unknown artist showed great skill in conveying the idea of something extraordinary in the air.

"Because of its comparative size," Magor says, "it is obviously not a bird. And just as obviously because of its shape (perhaps that is why he retained the winged look) it is not the sun."

Magor feels that the touch of real brilliance on the part of the Amerindian artist lay in the use of the four human figures. "Not only do they lend size and height to the object, but by their suggestion of a worshipful attitude, they create the impression that this was an event of rare spiritual importance."

Perhaps, though, the pictograph is not all that old. Could the Amerindian artist have been depicting his tribe's reaction to the first terrestrial aircraft which paid them a low, overflight visitation?

Magor answers this question by seeking out reference volumes which date the pictographs in the area as prior to *circa* 1860. Quoting from John Corner's *Pictographs in the Interior of British Columbia*:

"The fact remains that the Indians of the Interior Salish (whose territory included Christina Lake) and Kootenay tribes and their ancestors were productive painters of pictographs from some unestablished date until about 1860, when suddenly, and still unaccountably, the artists put aside their paints and applicators to paint no more."

In that same issue of *Canadian UFO Report* (Vol. 2, No. 6, 1973), Magor included an article from the *New Westminster Columbian*, in which staff reporter Alan Jay drew some rather astonishing parallels between the illustrations of "gods" and "visiting chariots" in Erich von Daniken's books and the rock paintings of the early Canadian Indians.

To quote an example from Jay's research: "A drawing photographed by von Daniken in the Sahara Desert shows a figure holding what appears to be a short rod totally enclosed in what the author claims is an

'PROPHESY IN STONE' – a petroglyph on medicine cave walls in Sedona, Arizona.

'E.T' petroglyph high on medicine caves in Sedona, Arizona.

early representation of a space-sphere . . .The Mara Lake (British Columbia) drawing shows a crowned figure holding two strangely shaped objects in each hand. . .The figure is totally enclosed in a sphere identical to the one depicted in the Sahara Desert drawing.

In one of his asides to reporter Jay's article, John Magor rightly reminds his readers that such interpretations can prove to be very tricky. For example, Magor points out, similar enclosures are seen around rock paintings where there is no hidden meaning. The early Amerindian artists had a habit of crowding pictures together on their painting surfaces. Enclosure of a pictograph may have been a means of avoiding confusion between the story of one painting and that of another.

There is another impressive similarity between Amerindian pictographs and "chariots of the gods" in the cone-shaped, rocket-like objects discovered near Cayuse Creek and Kootenay Lake. Quoting again from Alan Jay's article in the *Columbian*:

> Yet another rock painting at Cayuse Creek shows what is clearly a cone-shaped rocket with smoke and flame trailing behind it. And it contains a single humanoid figure apparently holding on to the inner wall of the rocket.
>
> A. . .pictograph near Kootenay Lake depicts the same kind of enclosed vehicle, also containing a single humanoid

Sherry Steiger at a sacred medicine cave in Sedona, Arizona.

Sherry captures a mysterious blue ball of light inside this prayer-healing sacred cave in Sedona, Arizona.

figure. The drawing also shows sections resembling the firing stages of a modern lunar rocket and two appendages closely resembling the retractable landing `legs' of lunar space module.

John Corner's book also shows pictographs of egg-shaped objects from which emanate wavy lines. Magor does not feel, as some interpreters have suggested, that these rock paintings depict the sun shining on water. The pictographs remind him of contemporary UFO descriptions of glowing, egg-shaped objects.

"The wavy lines underneath might have been the artist's way of showing the object was in motion," Magor theorizes. Or since early Amerindian craftsmen were meticulous about visual impression, the lines might indicate some kind of vapor trail.

In a Fraser Lake pictograph, there are no rays protruding from the upper surface, which, in Magor's opinion, "virtually eliminates any notion that the artist was drawing the sun." The more obvious Amerindian symbol of the sun was a circle with short straight lines emanating from the entire circumference. In the Fraser Lake pictograph, however, only zig-zag lines underneath are shown, "suggesting once more the idea of motion or propulsion."

Wisely, John Magor continually cautions his readers about ascribing to strange petroglyphs and pictographs depictions of early interactions between Amerindians and entities from "out there." There is one other petroglyph, however, which may bear enough circumstantial evidence to merit additional investigation – or at least theorizing.

At Roberson Point, Prince Rupert, there is an unusual intaglic (incised carving) of the outline of a human-like figure. In Tsimshian legend the petroglyph is known as the "man who fell from heaven."

John Magor comments: "Perhaps we can accept this as a literal definition. The carving is so utterly unlike anything else of early Indian origin on the West Coast that its history must be extraordinary."

Magor tells us that one theory has it that the Tsimshians who lived in that area might have one day returned to camp to find the body of an exceptionally strange man within their parameters. The considerate Tsimshians may have conceived the carving as an open grave to permit the stranger's spirit to return home. But if it is a grave, Magor reminds us, it certainly had not been intended for one of the Indians' own kind, for the practice among the northern native groups is to shelter graves, not expose them.

It would not have been at all remarkable for the early Amerindians of any tribe to believe that a stranger might have fallen to earth from the sky. Amerindians adhered to the universal belief which holds that the stars are the residences of spiritual beings who have a definite connection with, and a special relation to, human souls.

MEDICINE PRIESTS ARE THE WORLD'S OLDEST UFO EXPERTS

It turns out that the American Indian Medicine priests happen to be the oldest UFO experts in the world.

Dan Katchongva, a 109-year-old Hopi chief, has said that the frequent appearance of UFOs over the reservation in northern Arizona are in fulfillment of ancient prophecies.

According to Katchongva: "A petroglyph near Mishongnovi on Second Mesa shows flying saucers and travel through space. The arrow on which the dome-shaped object rests stands for travel through space. The Hopi maiden on the dome represents purity.

"Those Hopi who survive Purification Day will be taken to other planets. We, the faithful Hopi, have seen the ships and know they are true."

In 1984, Sherry was one of a few outsiders (i.e. non-Hopi) to partici-

One of Sherry Steiger's mentors and long-time friend, Rolling Thunder, the powerful medicine priest and spokesperson for the Shoshone and Cherokee tribes states: "There's order to all things in nature. The traditional way of life of the Native Peoples is part of the Creator's order, as is the way of the honeybee, the coyote and the eagle."

pate in a private kiva and kachina ceremony of the Hopi Elder Grandfather David.

She learned there that the Hopi's also talked of the "sky people" and the "star people" and of the very serious and important role that the Hopis believe these beings have held throughout time regarding the future of the Earth Mother and the fulfillment of prophecy.

Because of Brad's position of trust among native Americans, a Cherokee scholar confided to him:

"I don't believe that there is any doubt whatsoever that there are Indian people on the face of this Earth who did not originate on this planet.

"I tend to think that once the Hopi prophecies are carried out and their revelations are made known, they will bear this out."

A Cherokee physicist, who lives in Alabama, not only states that he has a recall of a past live in the Pleiades, he also says that he is able to fit his alien memories together with tribal legends that his people came from another world.

According to his past life memories:

> "We lived in domed cities with translucent walls. We could communicate with animals, transport ourselves instantly to other parts of our world.
>
> "My home was a place of golden color – a place of great beauty and calm.
>
> "I came with others to Earth to help it through its birth pains into an intergalactic community and oneness."

AMERINDIANS, UFOS, AND ATLANTIS

Sherry's long-term personal friendship with Rolling Thunder, the powerful Medicine priest and acknowledged spokesperson for the Cherokee and Shoshone tribes, expanded her awareness of the Amerindian-Sky People tradition.

Rolling Thunder has commented that certain scientists have said that those who are called "Indians" migrated over the Bering Strait from Asia. Others try to say that the Indians are one of the "lost tribes of Israel."

The Medicine Priest says that all of this is unnecessary conjecture, for the Amerindians know their own history very well.

"We were here when the Earth was young," Rolling Thunder states. "We are ancient on this land."

Rolling Thunder goes on to speak about ancient civilizations, pyramids, UFOs, Atlantis.

He seems to be echoing a growing number of Native American Medicine priests who say that now is the time to share information that was formerly known only to the inner circle of Medicine people.

CENTURIES OF INTERACTION WITH THE SKY BEINGS

It is always surprising to some people to learn that UFO contactees – those persons who claim to communicate with entities from outer space craft – have been with us for centuries.

While certain investigators have connected the "ancient astronaut" hypothesis to the wonders of Egypt, South America, and Asia, the discovery that the Amerindian tribes also interacted with the "Sky Beings" is quite revelatory.

In addition to the guidance gained from a telepathic transfer between tribespeople and their guardian star, several accounts suggest a much more physical interaction between the Sky People and the native people.

Numerous Amerindian stories relate the love affairs of beautiful Star Sisters and handsome Star Brothers with the tribespeople. Often, it is said, the Sky People descended to Earth in "large baskets" or "little moons."

In some instances, the Star Spouse comes and goes in the basket that appears in the magic circle.

In the case of the Star Wife, she may return with the result of their physical union so that the Indian father may meet his son who lives in Star Land with the great Star Chief.

Although there are accounts in the Amerindian legends of Sky People soaring off to the stars with a beautiful maiden who is never again seen by her tribe, most of the stories report that men and women are usually returned to their own kind *after* producing offspring, performing a requested task, or presenting a gift of Earth produce.

In the legends of Amerindians and the Sky People, nothing is forced and there are few accounts of violence between them. The only exceptions seem to arise in instances in which an Amerindian has been warned not to trespass in an area considered sacred to the Star People.

THE STAR WIFE OF WHITE HAWK (A Chippewa Traditional Story)

A young hunter named White Hawk was crossing a prairie when he discovered a peculiar circle upon the ground. The circle appeared to have been formed by a beaten footpath, and the curious hunter decided to conceal himself in the tall grass and learn what created the mysteriously trodden area.

After White Hawk had lain in wait for some time, he heard the sound of distant music coming from the air. His eyes we drawn to a cloud that was descending from afar. As it drew nearer, the hunter saw that it was not a cloud at all, but a basket device in which sat twelve beautiful maidens, each gracefully striking a drum. Soon the basket had settled itself in the midst of the magical circle. The instant the basket touched the ground, the young maidens leaped out and began to dance.

The young hunter was entranced by the beauty of their form and the grace of their dance. The drumming sound now seemed to be coming from the basket, and each of the young maidens struck a shining ball at each step. In his delight, White Hawk reached out to touch the dancer nearest him. But the moment the maidens saw him, they jumped back into the basket and were instantly drawn into the heavens.

The saddened hunter returned to his lodge, bewailing his misfortune. He complained to all who would listen how he had missed his opportunity to have a Star Maiden for his own. At night his slumbers were haunted by the sounds of the celestial music and the sight of the lovely maidens dancing in a whirling circle. He at last resolved to return to the

Sherry Steiger ponders the mystery of the strange vortex.

Brad Steiger at Medicine Wheel in Sedona, Arizona.

magic circle and wait until the maidens returned.

Secreting himself in the grass, White Hawk covered himself with the hides of opossums and patiently sat back to maintain his vigil. He had not waited long until he once again heard the delightful strains of the same sweet music. The basket was again descending from the stars.

When the Star Maidens were engaged in the movements of their dance, the man began stalking the dancer nearest him. But again they saw him and sprang for the safety of their basket.

The basket had only begun to rise out of his grasp when the hunter heard one, who appeared to be the leader, say, "Perhaps he has come to show us how the game is played by earthly beings."

But the others shouted, "Quick! Let us ascend!" They all joined in a chant, and the basket was almost instantly out of sight.

White Hawk's third attempt to attain a Star Maiden proved to be successful. This time, he disguised himself as a stump near the magic circle. When he jumped up and seized one of the Star Sisters, the other eleven fled to the rapidly rising basket.

White Hawk gently led the beautiful Star Maiden to his lodge, telling her how fine life was on earth. He treated her with so much kindness that she consented to become his bride.

Winter and summer passed joyously for the happy hunter, and his joy was increased by the addition of a lovely boy child to his lodge circle. But the Star Wife was growing weary with life of the tribal confines. She was a daughter of the stars, and her heart was filled with longing to return to her native land.

While her husband was away on a hunt she constructed a wicker basket inside the charmed circle, placing within it certain objects from the lodge as gifts for her father, the Star Chief. Then, taking her son in her arms and seating herself within the basket, she raised her voice in song and rose to meet a star basket, which took her to Star Land.

White Hawk was disconsolate with grief and spent many seasons sorrowing for his wife and son. At the same time, his son grew lonesome for his earth father. Grandfather Star Chief observed the boy's unhappiness and instructed his daughter to return to earth to invite White Hawk to come to Star Land and live with them. "But tell him that he must bring to me a specimen of each kind of bird and animal that he kills in the chase."

The Star Maiden did as she was told, and the joyful hunter gladly returned with them, bearing a large variety of game to present to the Star Chief. White Hawk's father-in-law was pleased by the gifts, and he prepared a great feast to welcome him. When the Star Maiden saw what

Rooms can be seen in these Indian ruins in Sedona, Arizona.

Ancient Indian cliff dwellings in Montezuma, Arizona.

joy could be had between the two races, she and her son agreed to return to earth with White Hawk.

THE LITTLE VANISHING PEOPLE

The magic circle of this Amerindian legend reminds us of the fairy rings, of which an ancient writer said: "They (the fairies) had fine music among themselves and danced in a moonshiny night, around, or in a ring, as one may see upon every commmon in England where mush-rooms grow."

The fairies, says another authority, referring to the Scoto-Celtic belief, are "a race of beings, the counterparts of mankind in person, occupations and pleasures, but unsubstantial and unreal, ordinarily invisible. . .noiseless in their motion. They possess magical power, but are mortal in existence, though leading longer lives than mankind. Nevertheless, they are strongly dependent upon man, and seek to reinforce their own race by kidnapping human beings. They are of a nature between spirits and men, but they can intermarry and bear children."

The Amerindians divided their supernatural visitors and companions into two categories, those glowing lights in the sky, the Star People, and those who inhabited field and forest, the *Puckwudjinies*.

Here we have one of those cross-cultural references which prove to be so thought-provoking. *Puckwudjinie* is an Algonquin name that signifies "little vanishing people." *Puck* is a generic of the Algonquin dialect, and its exact similitude to the Puck of the British fairy traditions is remarkable. Puck, or Robin Goodfellow, is the very personification of the woodland elf; he is Shakespeare's merry wanderer in *A Midsummer Night's Dream* – "sweet Puck," who declares what fools we mortals are.

Puck is no doubt derived from the old Gothic *Puke*, a generic name for minor spirits in all the Teutonic and Scandinavian dialects. *Puck* is cognate with the German *Spuk*, a goblin, and the Dutch *Spook*, a ghost. Then there is the Irish *pooka* and the Cornish "pixie." To break down *Puckwudjini* even further and concentrate on its suffix, we find *jini*, the Arabs' *jinni*, or genie, the magical entity of the remarkable lamp.

STAR PEOPLE AND
THE GREAT PURIFICATION

The majority of Amerindian Medicine People today believe that the Star People and the Spirit Guardians of the Earth Mother are becoming active at this time in an effort to aid humankind survive a coming Great Purification of the planet.

On August 2, 1974, during a lovely and meaningful ceremony, Brad was adopted into the Wolf Clan of the Seneca tribe by the Repositor of Seneca Wisdom, Twylah Nitsch. At a private ceremony, he was also initiated into the Wolf Clan Medicine Lodge. His name is *Hat-yas-swas* (He testifies), and he was charged with continuing to seek out and to share universal truths.

In October, 1974, Twylah received a vision about the role of the Medicine People in the coming days of strife, chaos, and cleansing.

"We are presently here because we are aware of the coming cleansing of Mother Earth," Twylah said. "Man has exerted an imbalance on her way of life; he has exhausted her natural resources. Medicine People must retain and guard the use of her gifts, or she will no longer be able to nurture her creatures. After the Earth Mother has been cleansed, Medicine People must seed the decrees of the Creator in the next world.

"When the transition occurs, our spiritual light will guide and protect us as we evolve as people of wisdom and as messengers of the decrees of the Creator. Each messenger, according to the level his gifts and abilities have developed, will assist others in seeking the Pathway of Peace."

Will there be assistance from other entities and intelligences from other dimensions of being?

"Yes," Twylah answered, "all over this world and on other worlds there are Messengers sitting in council. They will come to convene with us. This has happened before, and this communication will continue for time eternal."

RECEIVING A TEACHING VISION
FROM THE STARS

The following visualization may be read by a trusted friend or you may previously have spoken the process in your own voice and preserved the technique on a tape recorder. Be certain that you are at a time and in a place where you will not be disturbed for at least thirty minutes.

Your success in this exercise depends upon your willingness to permit a transformation to manifest in your consciousness. New Age music, such as that performed by Stephen Halpern or Michael Stern, can truly heighten the demonstration.

You may utilize any technique for quieting the consciousness that has been successful for you. Once the body has been relaxed, proceed with the following visualization:

You are gazing upward at the night sky. You begin to notice a particularly brilliant, flashing star high overhead. As you watch it, it seems to be moving toward you. It seems to be lowering itself to you.

Now you see that it is not a star at all. It is a large, beautifully glowing crystal starship. You feel no fear, only expectation. You feel secure in the love of the Universe. You feel unconditional love, as the object with the sparkling, swirling lights lowers itself near you. You know that it is a vehicle that has come to take you to level of higher awareness.

A door is opening in the side of the Crystal Light Vehicle. You look inside and see that it is lined with plush, soft velvet. You know that it is safe. You know that it is comfortable. And it glows within with the golden light of protection, the light of unconditional love from the very heart of the Universe.

Step inside, settle back against the soft, comfortable cushions. The door silently closes, and you know that the vehicle will now begin to take you to those higher levels of consciousness. You are completely comfortable, relaxed, soothed, but you know that you are being taken higher and higher, higher to total awareness.

You look out of a small window at your side, and you see Earth below you becoming smaller and smaller, as you rise higher and higher. Colors seem to be moving around you. Stars seem to be moving around you.

You feel love, pure, unconditional love all around you. You are being taken to a dimension of higher consciousness. You are being taken to a vibration of a finer, more highly realized, awareness. You know that you are safe. You know that some Benevolent Force is taking you to the Timeless Realm where visions live. You know that you will be safely returned to Earth once you have been to the In-Between Universe, the In-Between Dimension where teaching-visions await you. Colors swirl around you. Stars swirl around you. You are moving across the galaxy.

You are traveling higher and higher, higher into the very Soul of the Universe. You know that you will receive meaningful Teaching Visions when you reach that Timeless Realm where visions live.

And now your Light Vehicle has come to a stop. You look out your window and see that you have stopped before a beautiful golden door, a door that seems to be suspended in Space.

You know that when you step through the beautiful golden door, you will find yourself in the Timeless Realm where Visions await you. You know that you will have the ability to perceive and to comprehend

Kuichy points out the continuing use of land terracing developed by the pre-Incan Indians who were taught by 'starpeople' how to grow crops in this rugged vegetation.

meaningful teaching-visions, visions designed especially to provide you with deep and profound insights and understandings.

When you step through the golden door, you will enter a dimension which exists on a higher vibration. . .and your mind will be totally attuned to that frequency. You will have the ability to receive clear and revelatory visions. You will receive the answers to questions which you have asked for so very, very long.

When you step through that golden door, you will enter a realm where magnificent, colorful panoramas of living diagrams and teachings of awareness will be given to you. Unconditional love will permeate your entire being. Angels, guides, master-teachers will interact with you, share with you, teach you.

And now the golden door is beginning to open. A panel in your Light Vehicle is sliding back, permitting you to leave its interior, allowing you to step through the golden door.

You know that you are protected; you know that you are guided; you know that you are loved. You step from your Light Vehicle, and you step inside the Golden Door.

As you step inside, you know that you have the ability to perceive and to understand profound teaching-visions.

The FIRST LIVING DIAGRAM appears, sent to you by the Great Mystery. This living diagram explains to you THE TRUE NATURE OF THE SOUL. . .THE TRUE NATURE OF THE SOUL AND WHAT REALLY HAPPENS TO THE SPIRIT AFTER THE PHYSICAL DEATH OF THE BODY.

You are seeing now your true relationship to your Soul. . .your Soul's relationship to the Great Mystery. . .to the Universe. You are seeing yourself making the physical transition of death in a PAST life, and you see and understand what truly happens to the spirit at the moment of physical death.

Now your SECOND TEACHING VISION is beginning to manifest. The second living diagram explains to you, THE TRUE NATURE OF OTHER INTELLIGENCES IN THE UNIVERSE.

You may see alien lifeforms. You may be focusing in on a planet, a city, a people, a culture. . .all of which are alien to Earth. You are seeing an alien people. . .you are seeing their history, their customs, their belief structures, their methods of transportation.

Your THIRD LIVING, TEACHING-VISION is showing you scenes from FUTURE TIME. You are being shown THE FACE OF THE EARTH IN THE NEW AGE.

You are seeing this planet as it will look after the Earth Changes have fully taken place. You are being shown changes in society. . .art. . .politics. . .economics. . .clothing styles. You are being shown the skyline of cities. You will not be shocked by anything that you may see. . .even if cities are underground. . .even if new coastlines have been formed. . .even if new mountain ranges have appeared. . .even if new people walk among us. You will see and you will understand.

From the vantage point of looking backward from the Future, you will now see where the safe places will be. Look at a map of the United States. . .Canada. . .wherever you wish. The SAFE PLACE will glow with a golden energy. See and understand where the safe places will be.

And as you gaze into the FUTURE, you have the ability now to see an important FUTURE LIFE EXPRESSION OF YOUR SOUL. You are being shown an important future life experience that your soul will live on Earth. . .or elsewhere.

You have the ability to see yourself and to know what you are wearing. . .the color of your hair and eyes. . .whether you are male or female. . .or androgynous. You see your environment. Your domestic life-support systems. And you see WHO is with you from your present life experience or from any previous life experience.

And now your FOURTH LIVING DIAGRAM appears. You will now receive insights as to YOUR TRUE MISSION ON EARTH...WHY YOU REALLY CAME TO THIS PLANET IN THE FIRST PLACE.

You will be shown, and you will understand, why and when you first chose to put on the fleshly clothes of Earth. You will see and you will understand what it is that you are to accomplish in your Soul's evolution in this place of learning.

And now your CRYSTAL STARSHIP has reappeared. Once again, it appears to be solid around you. It has come to take you back to Earth Time, back to Human Time, back to Present Time, back to your present life experience.

You will remember all that you need to know for your good and your gaining.

You will be strengthened to face the challenges and the learning experiences of your life.

And know this: *The more you share your visions and your teachings, the more your understanding of them will grow.*

You are now awakening, surrounded by Light and by Love, by pure, unconditional Love. You feel very, very good in mind, body, and spirit. You feel better than you have felt in weeks, months and months, years and years.

You will awaken fully at the count of FIVE.

Chapter Six

ACHIEVING A BALANCE
WITH THE SPIRIT WORLD

In his *Narration of Habits and Customs of the Chippewa Indians*, Alexander McKenzie describes the Chippewa Medicine Priests who manifested Spirit entities in the phenomenon known as the "shaking tent":

> To these four spirits of the winds, the [Medicine Priest] appealed in his capacity of diviner and prophet. For them was constructed a lodge, in which was placed the presiding [priest], who on entering invited each spirit to receive incense from his calumet. When this invitation had been given, there was a silence among the people; they looked in the air to see the spirits come. The [Medicine Priest] sang, and a few chanters joined; the lodge shook; a noise and extraordinary confusion arose. It was thought to be the spirits, who were coming from the four corners of the earth. There were, besides the four spirits above named, four [entities] of lesser degree, making eight – a sacred number – who attended the [priest]. The first spirit to arrive was *Ackwin*, the spirit of the earth, who was the interpreting spirit. After her appearance, the four [spirits] previously invoked by the [Medicine Priest] made their appearance. Whenever a spirit arrived, a heavy blow was heard upon the ground, like the fall of some heavy article, and the lodge was rudely shaken. When the spirits were assembled, the council began. Speaking was heard in the lodge; there was much order in the discussion, the spirits speaking only one after the other, but each with a different voice. The people sat listening to these sounds in silent awe, and with fixed and breathless expectation. The sacred lodge was believed to be filled with spirits of omnipotent power, who had come, at the bidding of the chief prophet, from the remotest

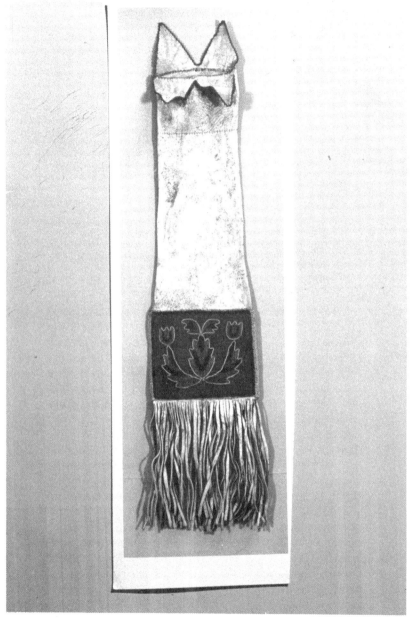

An ornate Chippewa Medicine bag with woodland beaded design, circa late 100s.

Inside one of the most sacred of the medicine caves in Sedona, Sherry Steiger felt this cave was used as a 'sweat' or sauna for cleaning and healing. The tour guide confirmed this to be true. Could the eerie reddish glow that appeared in developing the photo be enhancing this?

parts of the earth. And it was also believed that the [Medicine Priest] could send these agents to the uttermost bounds of the world in a few seconds, to do his bidding.

"To receive visions [beyond the vision quest experience] is a great thing," Iron Eyes Cody said. "But it is not always easy to have visions. I was in the sweat lodge a couple of years ago. My son was heating the rocks. A man passed out. My son was darn near passing out. Another man was coughing so that he couldn't sing with the rest of us. Then he saw his grandmother [that is, his grandmother's spirit form] in the dark place in the sweat lodge. Now, you have to believe this, because a vision is a matter of power of the mind. Visions come. You can see them. But you have to be strong-minded.

"A couple of months ago we had a Yuwipi meeting right here in the darkroom of my photography studio. We were talking about healing a woman. There were different ones here. Eagle Feather, the medicine man, came here to conduct the Yuwipi meeting. My wife was sitting next to the woman to be healed. The drummer was going; we were chanting.

"When we stopped, something hit my wife in the lap. When we turned on the lights, we saw that it was a bundle of feathers that had been on the other side of the room. Nobody could have gotten there to grab those feathers. Eagle Feather was by the altar in the middle. My son, Rocky Boy, and I were singing and drumming. Nobody could have got by us. The power of our Yuwipi happening made that bunch of feathers come and land in my wife's lap. After everyone saw what had happened, a lot of people told what they had felt and saw while we were in darkness. Magic is a strong power."

ESTABLISHING A DOORWAY
BETWEEN WORLDS

One of the primary essences of Indian Medicine is a strong belief in the partnership between the world of the physical and the world of the spiritual. If you begin your sittings out of a sense of levity, you are indicating your desire to fail at a most vital and serious project.

Some of you will probably achieve amazing results in a relatively short time. For others, the development of your powers may take weeks or months.

Take what comes to you, regardless of how small or irrelevant the manifestations may seem. Keep at it. Wait for better results. They will

This Sioux buckskin shirt with medicine charms is purported to have been worn by the great warrior-mystic Sitting Bull.

come if your perseverance and patience remain strong.

SET A REGULAR TIME

As much as possible, set a regular time for your development exercises. Don't overdo this by becoming a slave to the clock or by sitting too often.

Begin with ten-or-fifteen minute sessions every other day, or twice a week. Daily sessions are all right, too.

Gradually increase your time allotment to half an hour a sitting. Don't go beyond that unless and until you reach the stage where manifestations occur regularly and may occasionally require longer periods.

The time of day most suitable for your early exercises and, for that matter, perhaps for all psychic training and experimentation, is the latter part of the evening – when you are finished with the day's responsibilities, when your segment of the world has slowed down to a more serene pace.

The room in which you sit should be quiet, not too large, and sufficiently remote to assure privacy and safety from interruptions.

COMPLETE DARKNESS IS NOT NECESSARY

The lighting should be subdued. One bulb in a wall socket or a desk lamp is more than adequate – and even that should be shaded, possibly with a blue or purple scarf or some gauze of similar color.

Complete darkness is, of course, very desirable, as well; but sitting alone late at night in total darkness, attempting to make spirit contact, is often a bit unnerving for the novice. Let no one tell you that absolute darkness is essential to establishing contact with the world of the spirit grandfathers and grandmothers, the older, parental self within.

MEDICINE PRACTITIONER

If you are conducting your experimentations alone – which is not the most desirable arrangement except for the first part of your training – place yourself in a comfortable chair.

Sit quietly.

Divest your thoughts of your immediate worldly concerns and attempt to keep your mind blank.

Place yourself in as receptive a mood as possible. Be alert, but don't expect anything particular to occur. Be patient and wait.

If there seem to be points of light darting about the room, understand that they could be caused by natural manifestations or eye strain.

If you hear the creaking of floor boards, recognize that the sounds may be caused by changes in temperature rather than the appearance of an unseen spirit.

If your arms and legs become numb and cold, know that these sensations may be due to tiredness or rigidity, rather than the approach of the supernormal.

In other words, remain calm and don't become panicky or credulous. You will know well enough when the real thing comes.

Adjourn your expectancy sitting after ten or fifteen minutes. Repeat it a day later – or two or three days later – up to a total of a dozen times or more.

If genuine phenomena or raps do occur, don't be surprised and don't be frightened. Such things merely indicate that you are gaining in psychic strength.

You might obtain a large piece of natural quartz crystal to serve as your window into other dimensions.

If you use a crystal or a glass ball, place it on some dead-black material to eliminate glare, brilliant high lights, and reflections.

Make your mind a blank. Gaze – don't stare – steadily at the crystal, blinking as little as possible.

Don't permit yourself to become sleepy. Don't extend your steadfast gaze for more than five minutes at a time.

If your eyes begin to water, this may be taken as an indication that your time limit has been reached. You should then end your experimentation without delay.

If you are unable to see anything in the crystal, you can try to train your latent ability, or awaken and strengthen your visual memory, by first looking at a certain object in your own room and then trying to transpose it, mentally, into the crystal.

You might also close your eyes for a few minutes, think intensely of a person you know well, and try, with your eyes open, to see the picture of him or her in the crystal.

Not everyone is successful. Remember that, and don't be too disappointed if you are among those who lack this specific gift.

GATHERING A MEDICINE GROUP

Once you have begun to produce results in your experimentations, it is advisable to give up your solitary sittings and to work with one or more persons. Not only does this considerably lessen the danger of fatigue or boredom, which may cause you to give up too early, but it is undeniable that two or three people, even during the period of preliminary training, can accomplish more than the single experimenter.

You must be certain, however, that you have picked like-minded individuals to participate in your sessions.

For obvious reasons, you would not be likely to ask any friends who are hardnosed skeptics, who would not be able to recognize a miracle should one occur in their presence.

At the other end of the pole, neither should you invite friends who are "true believers." who would see a sign of the supernatural in every click of the thermostat.

It would be most desirable to choose friends who have an interest in psychic development, a good deal of patience, and a rather well-established sense of balance.

Once you have found the right person or persons, you can greatly vary and enlarge your training experiments.

To begin with, go once again through the exercises described in this lesson. Once your fellow sitters have experienced these sessions, you can proceed to simple experiments in telepathy.

SENDER/RECEIVER

Appoint one of you to be the sender (or transmitter) and the other the receiver (or recipient). If a third person is in your group, let him or her be the observer and recorder, alternating these roles among you.

Let us say that you begin by assuming the role of the sender. Seat yourself at a table, brightly lighted by a lamp placed somewhat behind you and shining directly on a piece of paper in front of you.

Your face should be turned toward the place where the receiver is seated, some distance away, with his back to you.

On the piece of paper before you, draw a simple figure, such as a circle, a cross, a triangle, and so forth. For your early experiments it is wise to agree beforehand on four or five such basic designs to be transmitted.

After drawing the figure, focus your attention upon it. Concentrate on it for a minute.

Then, mentally, will the recipient to receive the impression that you are transmitting.

The recipient, in turn, tries to keep his or her mind a blank. If he is also seated at a table with a piece of paper before him and a pencil in his hand, he may sketch the figures that he has mentally received from you. Once the impression is received, the recipient should draw it without hesitation, announcing when he or she has done so.

After some practice, the results you will achieve will be rather amazing. You will find that the number of correct impressions received will figure out to be much higher than they would if they were mere guesses. You will see them stretch far beyond the law of probability and chance.

THE CIRCLE

Once you have begun to work well together as a group it will be time for you to form your "Circle."

While there are circles designed for research and scientific exploration, the more successful groups are those composed of men and women who care about one another and who are in harmonious spiritual accord. It has often been observed that sympathy, earnestness and purpose, harmony, and patience are prerequisites to success in establishing contact with a dimension of greater wisdom.

How many people should belong to a Circle is a matter of individual preference. Two people may produce excellent results if they psychic talents have been sufficiently developed.

Through generations of experimentation, it has been set forward that four to six is a desirable number. Eight sitters seems to be the maximum number of seekers for the preservation of harmony and the elimination of discord.

Private Circles usually meet in the home of one of the sitters. The room set aside for the ceremony should be medium-sized, quiet, and so far as possible removed from street noises and other disturbances. It should be without a telephone, for nothing can be more disruptive than the sudden ringing of the telephone bell.

The room should be well-aired before the session begins. It should be comfortably warm, but not overheated. Smoking should be discontinued during the actual session. The consumption of alcoholic beverages before and during the session definitely should de banned.

Experience has shown that dry weather is best for the production of phenomena and that dampness or rain often hinder their occurrence. On the other hand, a sudden thunderstorm is very often conducive to the production of most unusual manifestations.

The best time for your circle to meet is some time in the evening after dinner. You should choose a convenient hour when each of your sitters has had an opportunity to permit the day with its worries and responsibilities to have receded a bit into the background.

It is important that you sit regularly and always at the same time and place. Twice a week is the maximum number of meetings for your Circle. A once-a-week meeting would be preferable.

Each individual session should last no longer than an hour. In the beginning of your sittings, it would be best to limit the sessions to about half an hour.

It should be understood from the very beginning that each person in your newly formed Circle must sit regularly and patiently for an absolute minimum of twelve sessions. When you have completed the last session in the first cycle, permit the individuals to decide whether they care to continue studying and sitting with you.

Never restrain those members of the Medicine Circle who become dubious or bored. You should replace them with new sitters as soon as possible.

The first time your Circle meets, you would be wise to select a leader to be in charge of the proceedings, to ask questions as soon as contact with the grandfather or grandmother manifests, and to time the sittings. It must be agreed by all that each sitter will obey the orders of the leader and abide always by his or her arrangements.

It might also be a good idea to appoint a recording secretary, who will keep the minutes of each sitting and who will be certain that appropriate music will be provided.

The leader should assign seats to members of the Circle, and once a seat has been assigned, it should be retained during the entire cycle of meetings unless developments unforeseen should make a change advisable.

The kind and intensity of light most appropriate for the development of phenomenon varies according to the psychic strength of the shaman and the sitters. The best authorities of the subject consider it a kind of general rule that a bright white light is definitely detrimental to almost any kind of manifestation.

Some Circles prefer sitting in darkness until the first unmistakable phenomena occurs. From that point onward, a dim light is turned on.

A calm state of mind should be preserved by all sitters. It isn't necessary to be overly serious or to be gloomy. Just be open-minded and relaxed.

Try to convince everyone that intense concentration should not be attempted. Tension, excitement, fear, nervousness, can be as great a hindrance to the proceedings as arrogance, skepticism, and levity.

Wait patiently for what may happen. Don't be overly critical of what may manifest in those early stages. It is best in the beginning to accept what occurs, rather than to make immediate judgments and attempts to interpret.

Don't expect miracles, the levitation of one of the sitters, or dramatic psychokinetic manifestations. This is real life. Your meeting has not been equipped with Hollywood-type special effects.

SPIRIT MANIFESTATIONS

When one of your Circle feels that a message from the older, wise self has occurred, be cordial to the entity. Welcome it warmly; speak to it confidently and calmly.

Prepare questions that you wish to ask beforehand. When answers do come, do not flatly contradict them and do not break into laughter and declare that such things are impossible.

Later, when contact is firmly established, it will become possible to question the higher levels of awareness and to ask them more completely to define matters.

All conversation with the older selves within should be carried on through the person chosen to direct the meeting. Close adherence to this rule will not only prevent mix-ups and misunderstandings, but it will contribute greatly toward a more rapid progress in your Circle's development.

Don't set out to achieve any particular kind of manifestations, such as spirit materialization. Take whatever comes, and try to go on from there.

The messages which you will receive will vary greatly in value and content. Sometimes they will be absolutely startling, sometimes trifling, sometimes obviously transmitted in an attitude of teasing and gentle raillery.

The time that will elapse before the first phenomenon occurs and the transmission of veridical messages (messages that can be substantiated and proved) of sometimes great length and importance will vary greatly from session to session. On occasion, manifestations will start as soon as the lights are dimmed and the Circle closed. During other sittings, the participants may not be able to get beyond the simplest phenomena.

Almost certainly, though, results will get better and better and gain in importance from sitting to sitting. With the necessary patience and perseverance, some results will be absolutely certain to come through to you.

THE SHAMAN

Perhaps when your new spirit Circle assembles for your first meeting, you may be uncertain as to which of your number is the best one to serve as the Shaman. After the first timid manifestations begin to occur, it may be desirable to establish who among you is the actual gifted one.

This can be easily accomplished by asking each member in turn, to leave the room. The moment the real Shaman has been eliminated from the circle, the meaningful contact will cease.

It is possible, of course, that more than one of your number is gifted.

In itself, the matter is unimportant. By the time that your Circle arrives at the more complex experiments, the question of who is the best Shaman will have been answered in a dozen different ways. The less powerful – and all members of the Circle – will serve the principal Shaman as "batteries" enabling your Circle to produce increasingly impressive phenomena.

TRANCE

Trance is a completely natural and normal state. It comes about in psychically gifted persons in order to facilitate their communication with the unseen world.

Since entranced people remember little or nothing of what takes place or of what they may say, it is important that the recorder of your Circle keeps careful written accounts of what has been uttered. Memory should not be relied upon.

Let us suppose that you are serving as the Shaman. Sit in the usual quiet room, holding hands with the person on either side of you. They, in turn, are holding hands with whomever is beside them, thus forming a circle around the table.

Sit for a moment or two listening to the restful music that should always ben played during your sessions. Take a few deep breaths, holding them comfortably for a count of three.

Wait patiently.

Call out in a quiet voice, whatever letters, words, images, symbols, or impressions begin to come to you.

The recorder should be writing down all utterances for later examination.

In all likelihood, your state of trance will become deeper with each word or image that comes to you. The heightened interest of the members of the Circle will give you additional psychic strength.

PHYSICAL PHENOMENA

If there have been indications during your earlier sittings that one or the other of your Circle may be developing the ability to produce physical phenomena, the leader of your group must instruct all members to observe strict rules of etiquette. At no time, it must be emphasized, should the one who is producing physical phenomena be touched during the trance state.

The phenomena that may occur are manifold. There may be levitation of objects, of the medium, or one of the sitters. Light or heavy objects may be moved by unseen hands.

Whatever happens, remain calm. Remember that no phenomenon is supernatural – only supernormal.

Chapter Seven

RESIST THE EVIL LORD
OF THE WILDERNESS

Father Marquette, the celebrated Jesuit priest-explorer, was among the first white men to view the startling murals that some artist from a forgotten tribal culture had painted on a high bluff of the Mississippi. The two petroglyphs, each about 30 feet in length and 12 feet in height, depicted two hideous, gigantic, winged monsters. In his journals of discoveries, published in Paris in 1681, the priest wrote:

"As we were descending the river we saw high rocks with hideous monsters painted on them and upon which the bravest Indian dare not look. They [have] head and horns like a goat; their eyes are red; [they have a] beard like a tiger's and a face like a man's. Their tails are so long that they pass over their bodies and between their legs under their bodies, ending like a fish's tail. They are painted red, green, and black. . . ."

The pious Marquette concluded that the paintings were of a diabolical nature. They reminded him, he said, that the "devil was lord paramount of the wilderness."

The two enormously large petroglyphs were clearly visible on the north bank of the Mississippi where the Illinois State Prison was later built at Alton. Traces of their outlines remained until the limestone on which they had been engraved was quarried by the convicts in about 1856.

Sometime in the 1840s, Professor John Russell of Jersey County, Illinois, set out with a guide to explore the cave on the north bank of the Mississippi River that various Indian tribes regarded as the lair of the *Piasa*, a gigantic flying monster with an appetite for human flesh.

"The roof of the cavern was vaulted," he wrote in his report. "The top was about twenty feet high. The shape of the cave was irregular, but so far as I could judge, the bottom would average 20 by 30 feet. *The floor of the cave throughout its whole extent was one mass of human bones.* Skulls and other bones were mingled together in the utmost confusion. To what depth they extended I am unable to decide, but we dug to the depth of three or four feet in every quarter of the cavern and still found only bones. *The remains of thousands of humans must have been deposited there.*"

Is it possible that the *Piasa* of Native American legend actually existed as a surviving Pterodactyl from the Age of Reptiles? Or was it, as one missionary suggested, the "twin brother of Satan"?

In his forty-eight page booklet, *The Piasa or The Devil Among the Indians* (Morris, Illinois, 1887), P.A. Armstrong described the creatures as having ". . .the wings of a bat, but of the shape of an eagle's. . . . They also had four legs, each supplied with eagle-shaped talons. The combination and blending together of the master species of the earth, sea, and air. . .so as to present the leading and most terrific characteristics of the various species thus graphically arranged, is an absolute wonder and seems to show a vastly superior knowledge of animal, fowl, reptile, and fish. . . ."

Whatever the petroglyphs truly represented, all the Amerindian nations of what then constituted the Northwest Territory had a terrible tradition which they associated with the monsters they called the *Piasa* or *Piusa*. The frightening creature was generally feared because of its propensity for snatching tribespeople and making off with them. Professor John Russell published an account of the Piasa's insatiable hunger for human flesh in the 1948 July number of *The Evangelical Magazine and Gospel Advocate*:

"[The Piasa] would dart suddenly and unexpectedly upon an Indian, bear him off into one of the caves on the bluff and devour him. Hundreds of warriors attempted for years to destroy him, but without success. Whole villages were nearly depopulated, and consternation spread through all tribes of the Illini."

At about the same time that the Piasa was preying on the Amerindians along the Mississippi, one of its cousins may have been snacking on the Mayans in Mexico. The November 1968 issue of *Science Digest* carried the startling thoughts of Mexican archaeologist-journalist Joe Diaz-Bolio concerning his discovery of an ancient Mayan relief sculpture of a peculiar serpent-bird. The sculpture was found in the ruins of Tajin, located in Totonacapan in the northeastern section of Veracruz, Mexico; and Diaz-Bolio theorized that the flying serpent was not "merely the product of Mayan flights of fancy, but a realistic representation of an animal that lived during the period of the ancient Mayans – 1,000 to 5,000 years ago."

According to the legends of the Indians of the Illini, it was a re-sourceful chief named Watogo, who after a month of fasting and prayer, received the instructions from the Great Spirit. These instructions enabled him to kill the fearsome beast. Watogo, willing to die for his tribe, presented himself as a victim so that his best bowmen could send poisoned arrows into the flying monster that swooped toward him. The Master of Life, in recognition of Watogo's generous deed, held an invisible shield over him, and the Piasa uttered a wild, fearsome scream and expired.

Although many traditional shamans recognized the existence of the so-called "evil lords of the wilderness," they believed such an evil spirit to be a mistake of the Master of Life. The following is a legend of the Algonquin as translated in the early 1800s by Mrs. E. Oakes Smith and adapted by us for purposes of illustration.

> Metowoc (Long Island) was formerly a vast level plain, that, having once been overwashed by the sea, was exceedingly smooth and seemed like a large, sandy table. It was upon this plain that the Master of Life worked out his creations undisturbed. Here he would frequently try his creations, and, giving them life, would set them in motion upon the island. If they did not suit him, he would withdraw their life from them before they escaped. There are now seen upon this island little lumps, or green tussocks, where the Great Spirit had commended some immense quadrupeds, and, finding them unsuitable for his purpose, had destroyed them on the very spot whereupon they had been formed.

> It was in this manner he constructed his animals: He placed four cakes of clay at proper distances upon the ground, and then slowly worked upward as one constructed a canoe. After the animal was finished, he dried it a long time in the sun; then, opening a place in its side, he entered it and remained many days. When he came forth, the shivering creature swayed from side to side, shaking the island by its motion. If its appearance was pleasing in his master's sight, he was allowed to depart upon the north side of the island, passing through the sea to the opposite shore.

> At one time the Master of Life occupied himself a long time in building a creature of marvelous size, which was an object of great curiosity to the little entities who often visited it. Notwithstanding the pains with which the Master of Life worked over the animal, it proved too large for his taste; besides, he was unwilling to give life to a creature that would have so much strength; and so he concluded to leave it where it was. Thus neglected, the weight of the monster caused it

partly to sink down into the island, where it hung supported by its head and tail.

After this the Great Spirit amused himself by making certain new creatures; but, on finding that they were not so attractive, he would receive their life into himself, then cast their bodies within the frame of the unfinished animal. In this way a great variety of oddly shaped things were hid together in what was called the Place of Fragments.

One day the Master of Life molded two pieces of clay into two large feet, like those of a panther. He did not make four; there were but two. He slipped his own feet within them and was pleased to find their tread was light and springy, so that he might walk with noiseless speed. Taking his feet out, he made a pair of very long legs. These he caused to walk.

Finding their motion was easy, he fastened upon them a round body, covered with large scales, like an alligator's. But the figure doubled forward, so the Great Spirit caught a black snake that was gliding by, fastened it to the body, and let it wind itself about a sapling near by – which not only held the body upright, but made a very good tail. The Great Spirit had made the shoulders broad and strong, like those of a buffalo, covering them with hair, and making the neck very short and thick and full at the back.

Thus far the Master of Life had worked with little thought; but, when he came to the head he reflected a long time. He took a round ball of clay into his lap, and worked it over with much care. Musing deeply, patting the while the top of the ball, he almost forgot the work to be done, for he was considering the panther-feet and buffalo-neck.

He concluded to make the eyes like those of a lobster, and then the creature could see on all sides. The forehead he made broad and low, and the jaws were set with ivory teeth, and were made heavy and strong, with gills on either side. The nose was like the beak of a vulture, and a tuft of porcupine quills made the scalp-lock.

Here the Master of Life paused. Holding the head out at arm's length, he turned it from side to side. He passed it rapidly through the air and saw the gills rise and fall, the eyes whirl, and the beak look keen; and he became very sad. He had never made such a creature – one with two feet who should stand upright and see upon all sides – yet he resolutely placed the head upon a pair of shoulders.

Night now approached, and with it a tempest arose. Heavy clouds obscured the moon, and the wind swept over the island in fierce gusts; the beasts of the forest began to roar, and the bats skimmed through the air.

A panther approached, and with one foot raised and bent inward looked at the image, smelling of the feet that were like his own. A vulture swooped down and made a dash at the beak, but the being brushed him away. Then came a porcupine, a lizard, and a serpent, each attracted by a likeness to itself.

The Master of Life veiled his face many hours, while the strong wind swept by him. Seeing that like attracts like, the idea grew into his mind that he would have some creatures who should be made, not like the things of the earth, but after his own image. Many days and night he reflected upon this.

He saw all things. Now, as he raised his head, he noticed that a bat lit upon the forehead of his image, its great wings spreading on each side; and he rose up, took the bat, and held its wings over the image's head. (Since then the bat, when he rests, hangs his head downward.) The Master of Life then twisted the body of the bat from its wings, having taken its life, by which means, as he held the bat over the image's head, the whole thin part of the bat fell down over its forehead, like a hooded serpent.

The Great Spirit did not cut off the face below, but went on, making a chin, and lips that were firm and round, that they might shut in a forked tongue and ivory teeth. He knew that, with the lips and chin, it would smile when life was given it.

The image was now entirely completed, except the arms; and the Master of Life saw that, with a chin, it must have arms and hands. He grew more grave, for he had never given hands to any creature; but he did not hesitate. He made the hands and arms very beautiful, after the fashion of his own.

The work was then finished, but the Master of Life took no pleasure in it.

He began to wish that he had not given it hands. Might it not, when trusted with life, create? Might it not thwart even himself?

He looked long at the image. The Master of Life saw what it would do, should he give it life. He knew all things.

He now put fire into the image, and a red glow passed through and through it. But fire was not life.

Terrible and fierce was its aspect. The lobster-eyes were like burning coals, and the scales of its body glistened with fierce light.

The Master of Life opened the side of the image. He did not enter.

By his command the image walked around the island so

that he might see it move.

He now put a little life into it; but he did not take out the fire. He saw that the creature's aspect was very terrible, but that it could smile in such a manner that it ceased to be ugly.

The Great Spirit dwelt long upon these things, and finally decided that such a creature – made up mostly of beasts, with hands of power, a chin lifting its head upwards, and lips holding all things within themselves – must not live.

Upon this decision he took the image in his hands and cast it into the Place of Fragments; but he forgot to take out the life.

The fall was great, and the creature lay a long time without motion among the discarded creations that had been thrown there lifeless.

When a long time had elapsed, the Master of Life heard a great noise in the Place of Fragments; and, looking in, he saw the ugly image sitting up, trying to put together the old fragments that had been cast within the cavern.

The Great Spirit gathered a large heap of sand and stones and closed up the mouth of the Place of Fragments.

The noise now grew louder. When a few days had passed, the earth began to shake, and hot smoke issued from the ground. The spirit beings of sea and land crowded to Metowoc to see what was the cause of the disturbance.

For the first time, it occurred to the Great Spirit that he had forgotten to take the life from the image he had cast within the cavern; and therefore, he came to watch the result of his mistake.

While he and the spirit beings stood close by the cavern listening to the noise, which continually increased, suddenly there was a great rising of the sand and stones. The sky grew dark with wind and dust. Fire ran along the ground. Water gushed high into the air.

Terrified by these signs, the spirit beings retired with fear. With a great, rushing sound, the image came forth from the cavern. His life had grown strong within him, fed by the burning fire; and at the sight of him every earthly creature trembling hid, while, filling the air with their cries, the spirit beings fled from the island shrieking:

"It is the Evil Spirit! It is the Evil Spirit!"

FACING THE DARK FORCES
OF NEGATIVITY

Although a belief in the existence of a personal devil is common in the religious concepts of humankind, the traditional Medicine people did not conceive of an omnipresent evil spirit that had been created by the Master of Life for the purpose of tempting humankind or of destroying it. As illustrated by the recounting of the above legend, they perceived the origin of the dread entity as a mistake of the Creator, which is probably as wise a way of quieting the haunting question of the origin of evil as that taken by many philosophers and theologians.

Dealing with evil and negativity is a great part of the challenge of walking in balance on the Earth Mother. Evil cannot be ignored, and it cannot be hidden. Neither can one run away from its poison and its deceit. The Dark Side of the Force must be confronted with discernment, discipline, and direct action.

BANISHING EVIL AND NEGATIVITY
WITH THE LIGHT OF THE RAINBOW

Here is a wonderful series of mental exercises which can prompt your own Inner Shaman to focus your spiritual resources and banish negative energy from your life. The technique requires that you visualize yourself drawing down all the colored rays of the rainbow as a focused light beam of transmutation. Some students have wished to employ a crystal as a kind of physical stimulus to prompt even greater concentration of energy, so we have included instructions which utilize a quartz crystal. Such usage of the gem is, of course, optional.

Visualize that your Spirit Guardian is at hand to direct the Rainbow Light of Transmutation. Proceed with the understanding that the complete spectrum of light in the rainbow has the power to assist you in balancing the negativity that you may have sown or that you may have directed against yourself. By earnestly manifesting the Rainbow Light of Transmutation, you will be able to eliminate any negativity in your life.

Hear your Spirit Guardian telling you that the Rainbow Light of Transmutation is like a cosmic eraser. When you learn to use it often and opportunely, you may erase from your spiritual spectrum all that is not of the Divine Light of the Master of Life.

Other Medicine teachers have said that the Rainbow Light of Transmutation may be used to dissolve disease, to eliminate suffering, to cure illness. Disease, suffering, and illness are all manifestations of chaos and discord. Suffusing them with the Rainbow Light may alter them and raise their vibratory levels to points of transmutation.

Know and understand that *you*, under the direction of your Spirit Guide, may use the Rainbow Light in a daily ritual of transmutation, thus removing all negativity and fear from your life.

Hold your crystal in your left hand, envision the Rainbow Light and ask that your Spirit Guide focus the energy through your crystal and permit the power to connect you to your higher self.

Visualize the light moving over you in a wave of warmth. See it touching every part of your body. Feel it interacting with every cell.

Say inwardly or aloud to your Spirit Guardian:

"Beloved guide, assist me in calling upon the highest of energies in the Source of All-That-Is. Activate my highest self to channel directly to Oneness. Stimulate the law of positive action for myself and all of us who stray from the light. Permit the Rainbow Light to move around and through me. Allow the transmutating energy to purify and to elevate all impure desires, incorrect concepts, anger, wrong-doing, improper memories and fears. Keep this light bright within me. Replace all negative, chaotic, fearful vibrations around me and in me with pure energy, the power of accomplishment, and the fulfillment of the Divine Plan of the Master of Life."

You may also utter this affirmation each morning upon arising:

"Beloved Spirit Guardian, I feel you on this new day, activating my higher self and charging me with perfect health, joy, love, the elimination of all fears, and the fulfillment of those physical things which I truly do need for my good and my gaining."

If you should feel discord coming upon you in a crowded place or in an environment wherein it is not immediately practical or possible to employ the Rainbow Light of Transmutation in an effective manner, do the following:

Hold your crystal in your left hand and cross your arms over your solar plexus.

Put your knees or your feet together. (If you are sitting, cross your legs.)

The above actions instantly symbolize that *you are not receptive to discord.*

If you are in a social situation and you feel that a person present is seeking to bombard you with negativity and discord –

1. *hold* your crystal in your left hand,
2. *move* your arms across your solar plexus,
3. *cross* your knees if seated,
4. *visualize* a cross of Rainbow Light dropping down from the heav-

ens between you and the person or the condition that is afflicting you with negative vibrations.

Such immediate action can block the vicious energy that is being directed at you. In addition, take short breaths for a time, inhaling shallowly, but exhaling in a somewhat forceful manner. This procedure should not be practiced over-long, but with ample time to express your sentiments that you are not even breathing in the negativity that is being broadcast in your direction.

Let us say that you have been bombarded with negativity by a cruel person or by a situation that has left you feeling rather defeated and very much alone in the world. Perhaps you are away from home, and you feel that everyone in that strange environment is against you.

Go to your room or to a place where you can re-establish your emotional and spiritual equilibrium. Sit quietly for a moment. If possible, play some soft, restful music.

After you have begun to calm yourself, take your crystal in your left hand and inhale, "I am." On the outbreath, say "relaxed."

Repeat this procedure a number of times. Take comfortably deep breaths. "I *am*," asserting your sovereignty and your individual reality on the intake: "*relaxed*" positively affirming your calm condition on the outtake.

Now gaze into your crystal and visualize someone who is extremely positive and who shares your philosophy, your perspective, your point of view about life and the cosmos. This may be a spouse, a friend, a business associate, a teacher.

See the person on whom you are focusing turning toward you with a smile of love. See the person extending his or her hand to yours.

Feel the touch of fingertip to fingertip. Sense the electrical crackle of energy moving between you. Experience the warmth of the love that flows from entity to entity.

Visualize your taking that person's hand in your own. Feel comfortable knowing that there is one who loves you and who exhibits concern for you.

See this shared love erecting a barrier between you and the negative bombardment to which you have been subjected that day.

Next image you or your friend reaching forth a hand to take another's. Visualize yet another like-minded man or woman who is being welcomed to your circle. See that person joining you, smiling as he or she takes a place beside you to add to your fortress of bonded energy.

Continue to visualize other men and women joining your circle until you have built as large a barrier as you feel that you need to face the hostility or the negativity that is being directed against you in this strange and unfamiliar environment. Feel strength, born of love, swell within your breast.

Visualize energy moving from member to member of your Medicine circle. See the Rainbow Light encircling your group externally. See the energy of unconditional love flowing from one to another as you envision yourself holding hands and linking your vibratory frequency to that of others of your spiritual philosophy.

After you have seen and felt the energy moving among your circle, visualize the power of the Master of Life descending from above and touching each of your members on the Crown Chakra. Feel yourself vibrating with the greatest emanation of love from the very heart of the Universe.

Hold this image and this energy as long as is needed.

When you have become completely fortified and calmed, it would be best to go to bed and enjoy a peaceful night's rest.

If this is impossible and you must return to the encounter, know that you will do so totally prepared and reinforced for any situation which might arise. Stride confidently into the "arena," knowing that you are linked together in an unbreakable bond of love with those kindred souls who share your perspective and your goals.

Chapter Eight

THE SACRED NUMBER FOUR

In the Far West, so say the old Dakota Medicine Priests, there is a splendid tent that rests upon a lofty mountain peak. Within the majestic tent dwells an expression of the Great Mystery known as the Breath Master. The tent has four openings, each guarded by a sentinel clothed in scarlet.

At the east is a butterfly, a winged fragment of a rainbow, representing the radiant marvel of dawn. The power and terror of the storms that come from the west is symbolized by the bear, a magnificent beast whose cunning and strength expresses the splendor of nature's awesome energy. A nimble-footed fawn is at the south; a fleet reindeer is at the north – swift messengers which complete the ever-turning wheel of the four winds. The Breath Master seizes the spirit of fire from the sun, controls the manifestation of light, rules the winds, and drives the breath of life into all living things.

The Winnebago place their spirit-deity Manabozho in the east, as the "white hare of morning." Manabozho also presided over the winds from that direction and attended the sun in its pathway across the sky. Animiki, spirit of thunder, stood in the west. Menengwa, manifesting in the form of a butterfly, ruled in the south. Mohokokokoho, represented as an owl, ruled in the north.

The number four is the great power number in Native American spiritual expression. To cite only one example, in rites of special worship, Medicine priests of a number of plains tribes used four sacks made of buffalo hide, shaped in the form of a turtle, elaborately sewn together, with a bunch of eagle's quills at the one end. The sacks were filled with water, and said to be drawn from the four directions of the Earth Mother and in the possession of the tribe since the settling down of the great waters at creation. Four shells were used for rattles in the mystic dance that accompanied the special rite.

In the Bible, the divine Urim and Thumim, by which God spoke to Moses, were the four rows of stones in the breastplate of his brother Aaron. The Moslems believe that the four angels Gabriel, Michael, Israfel, and Azarael stand in special favor with the Most High and participated in the creation of humankind.

Numerous scholars have observed that there appears to be a recognition of some universal law around the concept of using the number four in the most sacred acts of worship. It would seem that the number is very often made to typify the four points of the heavens and the human form. The emblem of the four outstretched "arms" or "points" also predates the Christian cross as a sacred symbol.

The following is how Twylah Nitsch, Repositor of Wisdom for the Seneca, explained the sacred symbolism of the number Four:

When the four ancient ones ascended in the Light to the Great Mystery, they learned that the symbolism of four was present in his extended hand. It meant life, unity, equality, and eternity. It also meant seeing, smelling, tasting, and hearing. These four senses could not function without feeling. Feeling includes touch and all emotion. When the hand is clasped, it is the symbol of unity. Unity is the spiritual law that binds the entire universe. They descended with a feeling of being completely healed of all the thoughts they had that were not right. From this experience they saw how the Pathway of Peace should be followed and how the great lessons should be learned. They learned at this time that self-knowledge was the key; self-understanding was the desire; self-control was the way, and self-realization was the goal.

They discovered that everything goes in a circle, and that communication is the key to the pathway of learning. They learned communication means understanding; understanding means peace of mind; peace of mind leads toward happiness: therefore, happiness is communicating. A circle again!

> And consider these symbolic representations of the
> number four:
> The first four Creations were Sun, Moon, Water, Earth.
> The four laws of Creation are life, unity, equality,
> eternity.
> The four seasons are spring, summer, fall, winter.
> The four directions are east, north, west, south.
> The four races of Creation are white, red, yellow, black.
> The four senses of feeling are seeing, hearing,

tasting, smelling.

The four guidelines toward self-development are
the following:

Am I happy doing what I am doing?

What am I doing to add to the confusion?

What am I doing to bring about peace and contentment?

How will I be remembered when I am gone – in absence
and in death?

The four requirements of good health are food, sleep,
cleanliness, good thoughts.

The four divisions of nature are spirit, mind, body, life.

The four divisions of goals are faith, love, work, pleasure.

The four ages of development are the learning age, the
age of adoption, the age of improvement, the age of
wisdom.

The four expressions of sharing are making others feel
you care; an expression of interest (everything in creation
has something to offer; listen and learn); an expression of
friendship (promotes spiritual growth); an expression of
belonging (sharing of goals toward a higher
spiritual growth).

"My grandfather, Moses Shongo, spent so much time breaking things down in fours," Twylah said." He taught me to do things in fours, and all my life I have done this. When I iron clothes, I iron in fours. I iron four things and put them away. Then four more. When I clean, I clean in fours. If I don't do things this way, I don't feel good. If I don't satisfy myself in doing something, I don't bother doing it. It is amazing how it works.

Unity is the great spiritual law Twylah reminds us, and we can break that down into four parts, as well:

1. Unity is going into the Silence in spirit, mind, and body.

2. It is a union through which all spirituality flows.

3. It is a goal towards communicating with all things in nature.

4. It is recognized by the intellect through the senses, through the emotions, and through impressions.

"Unity is the law of nature. I have known this since I can remember. Everything has its place, and everything works in unison. If you get in trouble, it is because you have created some static in this unified picture, You have only yourself to deal with. You only have control over yourself; therefore, you have to begin there. Equality to the Indian meant that everything in this universe had a place."

Chapter Nine

THE HEALING ENERGY
OF COLOR MEDICINE

The importance of color in the Native American's depiction of the world was second only to number and to geometric form.

Other ancient shamans believed that each major color consisted of seven elements: a physical or material element, a vitality-giving power, a psychological element, a harmonizing quality, a healing power, an inspirational element and a spiritual or higher-consciousness element. To develop harmoniously one was told to visualize the seven basic colors mentally every day to obtain the full benefit of their existence.

Oriental pundits viewed the seven major colors as an ascending scale in the evolution of humanity. According to their calculations we have passed through the red, orange, and yellow ray periods and are in the fourth or green epoch which will lead us to a higher period of growth and into the vibration of the beneficial blue rays from which we shall eventually pass into the ideal ethereal conditions of the indigo and violet rays. All these cosmic rays are said to emanate from the supreme White Light which is the source of inexhaustible energy, radiating as it does from the sun.

Eastern mystics associate color vibrations with the Chakras of the human body.

The Violet Chakra is located at the top of the head, the Indigo behind our forehead, the Blue within the throat where it regulates the thyroid gland, the Green near the heart and the Yellow, which controls the adrenal glands, the pancreas and liver, in the solar plexus.

The Orange Chakra is centered in the spleen and the Red at the base of the spine. Each Chakra is said to absorb a special current of vital energy through its particular color ray. The Orange Chakra for instance draws in *prana* or life energy from the sunlight and distributes it to all parts of the body. Directly associated with air intake, the activity of this Chakra is determined by the rhythm of our breathing.

Deep breathing is of incalculable value because it enables the body to draw in a considerable supply of physical prana which is not possible with shallow breathing.

"BREATHING" COLOR

As it is generally believed in mystical philosophies, the air we breathe contains a vital force, called *prana*. By filling our lungs and holding the breath for a few seconds, we can extract this vital force to benefit our physical and spiritual well-being.

To obtain the maximum physical and spiritual benefits, breathing should be rhythmic – inhalation and exhalation being of similar duration with a short pause between the two processes. To begin, inhale for a count of 12 pulse beats, hold the breath for six, and exhale for another 12 beats. With practice, you may feel like increasing the duration of each operation, but don't strain.

Yogis recommend the practice of the "complete breath," which brings our entire respiratory apparatus into use. According to scholar Keith Ayling, it is done in the following way:

> Standing erect, or sitting with spine straight, steadily in-hale through the nostrils, first inflating the lower section of the lungs, thus allowing them to push out the lower part of the diaphragm. Then, fill the middle part of the lungs to push out the lower ribs and the breast bone, and finally fill the upper area of the lungs to contract the lower part of the abdomen.
>
> Retain this breath for six pulse beats – no more to start – and exhale slowly, lifting your abdomen as the air goes out of the lungs. Even if you are not breathing color, this method of breathing will give you an appreciable lift.

"The secret of color breathing is to keep in mind the idea that you are inhaling the color you believe you need to restore your health," said Ayling. "As you inhale the yogic complete breath, you should visualize the air you are breathing as being tinted with the color you desire.

"In your mind's eye, follow the course of your tinted breath through your body. During the short retention period, imagine it is flooding the area you wish to improve.

"You can begin by using the white light, considered to be the most powerful healer of all, representing as it does the light of the sun."

COLOR HEALING

It is also of vital importance to concentrate on the area of your body that requires healing. Some color therapists advocate telling the affected part to heal itself. Speaking aloud can help; words have vibrations.

Some researchers have suggested that while inhaling you say the following affirmation silently to yourself:

"I project the white light (or whatever color you are using) through my body to aid me in restoring health, vitality, and youthful beauty to my entire system."

If you wish, you can repeat it aloud between the deep breaths and thus benefit from the verbal vibrations. Doing this for three minutes in the morning and three in the afternoon usually produces a surprising effect. But again, don't overdo it.

THERAPEUTIC FUNCTIONS OF COLOR

Here are some therapeutic functions of the various colors as shared by numerous shamans and mystics:

To attain a youthful figure and eliminate wrinkles and flabby flesh, concentrate on a **rose-pink**, the color of youth and restoration.

Blue is considered to be the universal pain killer. When inhaling this soothing color, you should imagine that it is flowing through your tissues, removing the poisons and revitalizing your body.

Blue inhalations can be used to alleviate sore throat, fever, and eye troubles. It is also recommended for convalescence.

If you have been ill, use both **blue and green** in harmony with appropriate affirmations. Should you feel lonely, depressed, or tired as is often the case after illness, you can visualize inhaling these two gentle, soothing colors, always remembering to fortify them with affirmations.

For lack of bodily energy, and for help on those days when you don't feel like doing anything, think **orange** – the vitality ray. For some, this may be the most important and effective color inhalation.

To obtain general good health and vitality, you can practice inhaling **red, rose**, and **orange**.

Red is said to be the easiest color to visualize. It also counteracts anemia.

Green is a sedative and relaxant. It overcomes the stress of daily living and induces a sense of peace.

Yellow stimulates the brain, the spinal cord, and the solar plexus.

Violet is said to help headaches and neuralgia. It also stimulates the pineal gland.

The **white light** is credited with having the power of universal regeneration. It can be visualized as a combination of all other rays.

Color breathing can play a vitally important role in our daily lives.

If you are habitually depressed and gloomy, you should try inhaling all the rays in turn, the first in the morning after waking. Do the same for five minutes before going to sleep.

Watch carefully for the results and gradually eliminate the inhalation of one ray each day, in order to discover the most beneficial. In the morning, always end with deep inhalations of the **yellow ray**. Once you have discovered the ray which seems most beneficial for you, continue to inhale it, using an appropriate affirmation to help to change your outlook on life.

If you need more money, breathe deep, **rich green** to help banish your poverty vibrations – for that's what ails you. The green vibrations will attract what you need and want – money, friends, love, material comforts.

By affirming the benefits you are acquiring as you inhale the green ray, your life will change. Your consciousness will become rich and your personality magnetic. The ancients hailed green as the blessing of plenty.

The following are some general rules to help you obtain the fullest benefits from color breathing:

Banish from your mind all thoughts of illness, trouble, fear, and limitation. In particular, don't think of what ails you by name. Think of your mind as the **sun** of your body. Think strong, creative, and good thoughts about yourself.

See yourself in the state of health you desire. Use your own affirmation – and believe in it. Realize that you will definitely receive your supply of the cosmic healing force.

A COLOR MEDITATION
TO BALANCE YOUR ENERGIES

Visualize that at your feet lies a blanket the color of **ROSE**. The color of rose stimulates natural body warmth and induces sleep. It also provides one with a sense of well-being and a great feeling of being loved.

Now you see that blanket is really a kind of auric cover, a rose-colored auric cover. Imagine that you are willing the blanket-like aura of rose to move slowly up your body. Feel it moving over your feet, relaxing them; over your legs, relaxing them; over your stomach, easing all tensions; moving over your chest, your arms, your neck.

Now, as you make a hood of the rose-colored auric cover, imagine that the color of rose permeates your psyche and does its part in activating your ability to balance all your body's energy levels. Once you have done this, visualize yourself bringing the rose-colored aura over your head.

The color **GREEN** serves as a disinfectant, a cleanser. It also influences the proper building of muscle and tissue.

Imagine that you are pulling a green, blanket-like aura over your body. Feel it moving over your feet, cleansing them; feel it moving over your legs, healing them of all pains. Feel it moving over your stomach, ridding it of all pains. Feel it moving over your chest, your arms, your neck – cleansing them, healing them.

As you make a hood of the green-colored auric cover, imagine that the color of green permeates your psyche and does its part in activating your ability to regenerate all parts of your physical body. Once you have done this, visualize yourself bringing the green-colored aura over your head.

GOLD has been recognized as a great strengthener of the nervous system. It also aids digestion and helps you to become calm.

Visualize now that you are pulling a soft, beautiful golden aura slowly over your body. Feel it moving over your feet, calming you. Feel it moving over your legs, relaxing them. Feel it moving over your stomach, soothing any nervous condition. Feel it moving over your chest, your arms, your neck.

As you make a comfortable hood of the golden aura, imagine that the color of gold permeates your psyche and strengthens your nervous system so that your body-brain network will serve you to better become a practitioner of Medecine Power. Once you have done this, visualize yourself bringing the gold-colored aura over your head.

Researchers have discovered that **RED-ORANGE** strengthens and cleanses the lungs. In our modern society with its problems of pollution, our lungs become fouled whether we smoke cigarettes or not. Yogis and other masters have long known that effective meditation, effective altered states of consciousness, can best be achieved through proper techniques of breathing through clean lungs.

Visualize before you a red-orange cloud of pure oxygen. Take a comfortably deep breath and visualize some of that red-orange cloud moving into your lungs. Imagine it travelling through your lungs, cleaning them, purifying them, bearing away particles of impurities.

Now, visualize yourself *exhaling* that red-orange cloud of oxygen from your lungs. See how soiled with impurities it is. See how darkly colored it is.

Take another comfortably deep breath. See again the red-orange cloud of pure, clean oxygen moving into your lungs. See the red-orange cloud purifying your lungs of the negative effects of exhaust fumes, smoke, industrial gases. Exhale the impurities, then breathe again of the purifying, cleansing red-orange cloud.

YELLOW-ORANGE will aid oxygen in moving into every organ and gland of your body, purifying them, cleansing them. Imagine before you now a yellow-orange cloud of pure oxygen.

Take a comfortably deep breath and inhale that cleansing, purifying yellow-orange cloud into your lungs. Feel the yellow-orange cloud moving through your body. Feel it cleansing and purifying every organ. Feel it cleansing and purifying every gland. If you have *any* area of weakness or disease *anywhere* in your body, feel the yellow-orange energy bathing it in cleansing, healing vibrations.

As you exhale all impurities and inhale again the pure, clean yellow-orange cloud of oxygen, visualize the cleansing and healing process throughout your body. As you exhale and inhale, see your body becoming pure and clean. See now that the cloud that you exhale is as clean and pure as that which is being inhaled. You have cleansed and purified your lungs. You have cleansed, purified, and healed all of your body and all of its organs.

The color of **VIOLET** serves as an excellent muscle relaxant. Violet is a tranquilizer. It is a color of the highest vibration.

Imagine that you are pulling a violet, blanket-like aura over your body. Feel it moving over your feet, relaxing them. Feel it moving over your legs, relaxing them, soothing them. Feel it moving over your stomach, removing all tensions. Feel it moving over your chest, your arms, your neck – tranquilizing them, relaxing them.

Now, as you fashion a hood of the violet-colored auric cover, imagine that the same color of violet permeates your psyche and does its part in activating your ability to use true magic. Feel the color violet attuning your psyche to the highest vibration. Feel the color violet connecting your psyche to the God-energy. Once you have done this, visualize yourself bringing the violet-colored aura over your head.

BLUE is the color of psychic ability, the color which increases visionary potential.

Visualize a blue blanket-like aura beginning to move over your body. Feel it moving over your feet, relaxing them. Feel it moving over your legs, soothing them. Feel it moving over your stomach, your chest, your arms, your neck – soothing them, relaxing them.

As you make a hood of the blue-colored auric cover, imagine that the color of blue permeates your psyche and does its part in activating your ability to meet the spiritual guide who can most completely assist you in achieving the most important acts of Medicine. Once you have done this, visualize yourself bringing the blue-colored aura over your head.

You are now lying or sitting there totally wrapped in your blue-colored auric cover. You are very secure, very comfortable, very relaxed. Your mind is very receptive, very aware. You feel attuned with a Higher Consciousness. You feel as though your awareness has been expanded. You know that all of your energies of mind, spirit, and body have been balanced.

TWYLAH NITSCH'S REVELATION OF THE PATHWAY OF PEACE

The first stepping stone, the Blood-stone, glows in radiant shades of red. It plants the seed that awakens the seeker to the spiritual way of faith and beckons the seeker to the entrance of the Pathway of Peace.

The Blood-stone has seven facets. Each facet designates one of the spiritual senses of sound, sight, scent, taste, touch, awareness, and emotions. Standing upon the first stone is symbolic of the life materialized in the physical world and is a daily venture in faith.

The seeker learns that the Great Mystery, the Spiritual Essence, is connected with all things in creation and that all things in creation are connected with one another. It is the impressions influenced by this interconnection that affect the experiences in all creation.

The radiance of the Blood-stone flows throughout the seeker and into the material world, uniting all creation into thoughts and feelings of faith.

Becoming aware of the existence of the first stepping stone and the lessons it imparts opens the way to the second stepping stone on the Pathway of Peace.

The second stepping stone, the Sun-stone, glows in radiant shades of yellow. It plants the seed that awakens the seeker to the spiritual way of love, and it beckons the seeker to dwell upon the Sun-stone on the Pathway of Peace.

The Sun-stone has the same seven facets that designate the powerful spiritual senses of sound, sight, scent, taste, touch, awareness, and emotions. Standing upon the Sun-stone is symbolic of the life materialized in the physical world and is a daily venture in love

Its radiance of love flows throughout the seeker and into the material world. Faith and love go hand in hand. It is the spiritual expression of faith and love that makes the world go around and helps the seeker to grow in peace and harmony.

Becoming aware of the existence of the Sun-stone and the lessons it imparts opens the way to the third stepping stone on the Pathway of Peace.

The third stepping stone, the Water-stone, glows in radiant shades of blue. It plants the seed that awakens the seeker to the spiritual way of cleansing and soothing, and it beckons the seeker to dwell upon the Water-stone.

The Water-stone has seven facets. Each facet designates one of the spiritual senses of sound, sight, scent, taste, touch, awareness and emotions.

Standing upon the Water-stone is symbolic of the life materialized in the material world and is a daily venture of cleansing and being soothed.

The radiance of the Water-stone flows throughout the seeker and into the material world, nourishing it with cleansing purity. It is the fluid property that unites all creation into the stream of spirituality and helps the seeker to grow toward peace and harmony through its expression of peaceful relaxation.

Becoming aware of the existence of the Water-stone and the lessons it imparts opens the way to the fourth stepping stone on the Pathway of Peace.

The fourth stepping stone, the Fertility-stone, glows in radiant shades of green. It plants the seed that awakens the seeker to the spiritual way of abundance and renewal, and it beckons the seeker to dwell upon the Fertility-stone.

The Fertility-stone has seven sides, each designating one of the spiritual senses of sound, sight, scent, taste, touch, awareness, and emotions.

Standing upon the Fertility-stone is symbolic of the life materialized in the material world and is a daily venture in physical and natural growth. Its radiance flows throughout the seeker and into the material world, nourishing it with abundant life.

It is the renewing properties of the fourth stepping stone that unites all creation into environmental awareness and helps the seeker grow toward peace and harmony.

Becoming aware of the existence of the Fertility-stone and the lessons it imparts opens the way to the fifth stepping stone on the Pathway of Peace.

The fifth stepping stone, the Blossoming-stone, glows in radiant shades of coral pink. It plants the seeds that awaken the seeker to the spiritual way of upliftment, and it beckons the seeker to dwell upon the fifth stepping stone on the Pathway of Peace. The Blossoming-stone has the same powerful facets as the previous stepping stones.

The radiance of its unfolding properties flow throughout the seeker and into the material world, nourishing it with beauty and spiritual insight.

Standing upon the Blossoming-stone is symbolic of the life materialized in the physical world. It offers a daily venture in intuitive impulses and is a gift received on the Pathway of Peace.

Its properties of upliftment help the seeker grow toward peace and harmony.

Becoming aware of the existence of the Blossoming-stone and the lessons it imparts opens the way to the sixth stone on the Pathway of Peace.

The sixth stepping stone, the Charity-stone, glows in a radiant burst of spiritual light. It plants the seed that awakens the seeker to the spiritual way of benevolence in thoughts and deeds, and it beckons the seeker to dwell upon the sixth stepping stone on the Pathway of Peace.

The Charity-stone has the same powerful facets as the stepping stones that preceded it.

The radiance of the Charity-stone flows throughout the seeker and into the material world, nourishing it with acts of kindness and understanding.

It is the charitable properties of the sixth stepping stone that unite all creation into the ways of Spiritual Harmony. Its brilliance crystallizes the highest spiritual self in preparation for entering the Great Silence.

Becoming aware of the sixth stepping stone and the lessons it imparts opens the way to the seventh stepping stone on the Pathway of Peace.

The seventh stepping stone, the Healing-stone, glows in radiant shades of lavender. It plants the seed that awakens the seeker to the spiritual way of healing – the highest creative spirituality. It beckons the seeker to dwell on the seventh stepping stone on the Pathway of Peace.

The radiance of the Healing-stone projects the powerful facets in sound, in sight, in scent, in taste, in touch, in awareness, and in emotions, and it flows into the seeker and into the material world, nourishing all creation with the Essence of Spiritual Healing that leads toward peace and harmony.

The healing properties unite all creation into spiritual attunement, which flows throughout Eternity.

Becoming aware of the existence of the seventh stepping stone leads to the threshold of the Great Silence that opens the way of Spiritual Peace and Harmony.

> In the Silence
> All creation unites and communicates
> The Spiritual Way.
> Where life is pure, life is fulfilling;
> Life is understanding; life is sharing;
> Life is abundant; life is unity; and
> Life is Eternity.
> The ecstasy of Spiritual Enlightenment.
>
> As the seeker descends the Pathway of Peace –
>
> The seventh stepping stone reveals Spiritual Healing.
> The sixth stepping stone reveals Spiritual Charity.
> The fifth stepping stone reveals Spiritual Insight.
> The fourth stepping stone reveals Spiritual Awareness.
> The third stepping stone reveals Spiritual Cleansing.
> The second stepping stone reveals Spiritual Love.
> The first stepping stone reveals Spiritual Faith.
>
> The Light of all Light,
> The Light of all Faith and Love,
> The Light of all Knowledge and Inspiration,
> The Source of all Creation –
> The Spiritual Revelation.

RAINBOW CLOUD HEALING TECHNIQUE

Use any successful technique of your own to place yourself in a deep level of consciousness. Have someone read the following suggestions to you, or prerecord the suggestions and serve as your own guide via cassette tape.

You are so peaceful, so beautifully relaxed. You glance up into the blue, blue sky and pick the most attractive cloud that you can see. It is a rather small cloud, but it is exquisitely formed. It is a beautiful cloud with magnificent peaks.

You feel deeply at peace, looking upward at the cloud's fluffiness, its thick, rich fullness. It is soft and white, and it appears to be glowing...as it catches the rays of sunlight and shines with beautiful, prismatic colors.

As you watch the cloud, you wish to ride upon it, knowing that this special cloud would hold you safely in space. If you mounted the cloud, you would then be able to soar above the trees, the towns, the cities, Earth itself. You would be able to move into the heavens themselves. You could enjoy the beauty of the twinkling stars.

You could move so close to the stars. It would be as if you might reach out and touch them. As you move higher, the air would be fresh and pure. It would be a new world, a higher dimension. All would be so wonderful.

The cloud appears to be growing larger and larger. . .larger still. And you notice that it appears to be floating toward you. You are happy inside. Perhaps the Sky Father heard your wish, for the cloud is lowering itself to you. You know that you will soon be able to climb aboard.

The cloud settles down right next to you. You know that you may now climb safely aboard.

You easily step over a full, puffy rim into the soft, fluffy center of the cloud. It is so comfortable on the cloud, so peaceful. And you can lie back as if you are lying down in an incredibly comfortable reclining chair.

Your cloud is so soft, so strong, so secure.

A ray of light shines forth from the heavens and touches your strong and fluffy cloud. It causes your cloud to glow softly. The radiance is different from any other light that you have ever seen. You can feel it as well as see it. It feels strangely wonderful, and it causes you to become very happy within yourself.

You know that you have felt this sensation before. Sometime before in your life it has touched your heart. It is the warmth of love. . .a beautiful, gentle love. You feel so at peace, so happy, so loved. You begin to rise. . .floating slowly, gently, so very safely.

You know that you are protected by love from a higher power.

You begin to drift. . .drift and float. . .gently bobbing along like a cork in a pond. Drifting and floating. Drifting and floating. Drifting and floating. Higher and higher still.

As you drift. . .drift and float, you glance easily down toward the Earth. You can see the trees. . .the countryside. . . the cities and towns growing smaller and smaller until they look like tiny toys on a green blanket.

You are rising higher and higher, far above the ground. Smell the fresh winds as the air becomes fresher, cleaner, the higher you go. You breathe deeper and deeper, deeper and deeper, and you settle back comfortably on your cloud to rest and to enjoy the feelings of peace and of love all around you.

You are floating higher, higher, and higher. You are floating out of this time, out of this place, far out into the dimension from whence came that ray of beautiful light that made your cloud glow. You are going to that place in space where the warm, glowing light emanates.

There is an opening ahead, and it is coming closer and closer. You slip through the opening.

You can see now that it is not merely an opening, but a tunnel, a tunnel filled with myriad designs. And there is a light at the far, far end. See the light far ahead at the end of the tunnel.

Now you are speeding to the light. You are moving to that place in space where there is no time at all. You are coming swiftly to the end of the tunnel, and you slip easily through it into a strange and glorious place. This is a place that exists beyond time.

Concentrate on the area of your body that is painful, diseased, or malfunctioning. See in your mind that particular body part about which you desire to know more.

You have the ability to see all that transpired to cause the problem that so troubles you. See it. Know it. Understand it. Remember it. (Permit yourself approximately two minutes to contemplate your images and memories.)

Now you understand why you are suffering this problem. You see and know why the problem has come about. You are happy to have discovered where its roots lie.

And now, with the vibrations of this awareness, and with firm resolve to right all wrongs, to better existing circumstances, you are strengthened and know that you can be healed. You are wiser and stronger now, and you know deep within your heart that you can be released from the grasp of this event. You can be healed.

You glance down toward the east where a light, misty rain is falling, and you watch the sunlight sparkle through the tiny raindrops, which are transformed as if by magic into a myriad of sparkling diamonds. A beautiful rainbow appears, a rainbow that you know can heal you. The rainbow is formed from the colorful, prismatic glitter. See the stretching bands of lilac, rich lilac; rose, soft, beautiful rose; green, vibrant green; and sparkling, glowing gold before you. So beautiful. So near you.

You desire to pass through the healing rainbow upon your cloud and to feel the colors move all around and through you. You are going closer now, closer and closer. The rain has ceased, but the rainbow remains crisp and clear. You will start with the bottom color of gold and work up through all the colors to lilac.

You are passing through the **gold** – a glowing, sunny gold that touches your very being. You breathe much more deeply now, more freely now, as gold enters your body. You can see it all around you, glowing, warm and glowing. Gold is all around you and through you. Gold is going through you and you feel love enter your heart, mind, and body. You are now leaving gold and you enter into green.

Green – a very rich, living, healing green. Green as a fresh leaf. Feel and see the green all around you. Green, passing through you, healing your scars, wounds, pains, and troubles. A warmer loving sensation fills your being, and you leave green and pass into rose.

Rose – a delicate shade of rose, a pinkish shade of rose, so lovely, so beautiful. Rose all around you. Rose passing through you. You feel your heart being bathed in rose. Your heart is softer now, more pliable now, expanding and filling with an even richer, more beautiful love. You are leaving rose now and passing into velvety lilac.

Lilac – beautiful shade of lilac is passing through you. You feel yourself glow lilac, as you body is growing stronger and stronger, your love is growing deeper and deeper.

You are passing out of the lilac and leaving the rainbow. Before you, beaming down from the heavens is a rich, elegant shade of **violet**. Bright, glowing violet that is pulsating with life. Yes, the universal life-force is reaching down to you from the sky. It is touching your body.

You see **violet**, bright, glowing, pulsating all around you and you feel it within you. Violet is pulsating through your entire being. You can feel the life-force within you, and it feels so wonderful, so powerful, so beautiful, so good.

You are beginning to descend. Your cloud is beginning to descend, going down, down, down. Back to Earth. You will remember all that you have seen, realized and experienced.

On the count of six, all of your six senses will awaken and be made more perfect. **One,** your sense of taste. . .**Two,** your sense of smell...**Three,** your hearing. . .**Four,** your touch. . .**Five,** your sight. . .**Six,** the most important of all, your intuition, your Higher Self, now awakens. Awake, refreshed, positive, healed, balanced, and filled with love for all.

Chapter Ten

CRYSTALS, STONES, AND GEMS – SHAMANIC TOOLS

Toward the coming of the sun
There the people of every kind gathered,
And the great animals of every kind....
Verily all gathered there together,
By what means or manner we know not.

Verily one alone of all these was the greatest,
Inspiring to all minds, the great white rock,
Standing and reaching as high as the heavens,
enwrapped in mist,
Verily as high as the heavens.
Thus my little ones shall speak of me!

Hartley Burr Alexander tells us in *The World Rim* that these lines are from the ritual of the *Pebble Society* of the Omaha, whose emblem was a white or translucent pebble, symbol of the primeval waters from which the Rock of the World emerged, and potent as a vision-inducing charm.

"Mystically 'shot' with the pebbles, which were part of the `medicine' of the society, the members fell into trance, which in Indian lore is the road of understanding and of insight into things unseen," Alexander writes. "The practice suggests the custom, widespread in Indian America, of employing transparent or translucent stones – rock crystal, quartz, obsidian, and the famous greenstone of the south – as talismans and as inducers of vision."

Years ago when Twylah asked Brad if he had his Medicine stone with him, he reached into a pocket, brought forth the small, oblong stone which he carried at that time.

"My daughter Julie gave this to me when she was four years old," he said. "She had been outside somewhere, and when she came back into the house, she presented this rather uniquely shaped stone with the announcement that it was to be mine. Since she was at that possessive-ownership age, I assumed something pretty heavy must have told her that this was to be my Medicine stone."

Twylah took his stone, held it thoughtfully in an open palm. "Yes, I am sure that this is your stone. But let us find another for you."

She took two rather large bags from a closet of the longhouse workshop. "Here," she said, dumping their contents on the floor, "choose your stone from among these. Pass your hand over them until one sends out the vibration that it is yours."

"Open yourself," Twylah admonished. "Open up and let the stones speak to you. When you have selected a stone, I shall read it for you.

"The foundation of the universe is a stone. A stone is a common denominator of the universe. You can find one wherever you go. A stone has form and spirituality. Even the uninitiated have feelings for stones, whether they realize it or not. When this Earth is cleansed, it will be the stone that will be the nucleus and expand or contract. The Indians have a beautiful philosophy that revolves around the stone, and it has almost been lost.

"The Indians did not worship the stone. The Indian used the stone to remind him of the oneness of all creatures of the universe and that the same spiritual energy flows through all things."

THE INCREDIBLE MEDICINE
OF STONES AND GEMS

"Amulets can bestow complete control of the material plane and destiny; perhaps this explains why this knowledge has been forbidden for the uninitiated down through the centuries," Rev. Richard De A'Morelli explained. "Magical gems are not and can not be intended for use by the careless or foolish at heart."

Perhaps the most popular amulets are the twelve birthstones. Because most people are familiar with these stones, the powers of each will be considered.

Diamond – This precious gem is associated with the sign of Aries. A diamond amulet traditionally symbolizes enduring love and happiness in a marriage. Given as a gift, the gem strengthens emotional bonds and promotes loyalty.

A diamond pendant may be worn to obtain honor and friendship.

Mounted in a ring, the amulet insures lasting marriage and financial success.

Emerald – Traditionally associated with the sign Taurus, this precious green gem has several unique properties.

An emerald pendant affords women protection against rape and defilement. Mounted in a ring, the stone promotes domestic stability and fortune.

According to the legend, this amulet may be used to combat epilepsy, depression, and insanity.

Agate – This stone may appear as stripped or clouded quartz, and is astrologically associated with the sign Gemini.

An agate amulet worn as a pendant promotes good health and fertility.

An agate ring bestows wealth and honor; also, it can be used to obtain favors from people in high positions. Legend has it that any person who gazes upon this charm will be compelled to speak the truth and cannot maintain secrecy.

Ruby – This popular birthstone, which is associated with the astrological sign Cancer, reputedly promotes mental health and tranquility.

A ruby pendant combats depression and enables the wearer to overcome sorrow. A ruby amulet worn as a ring bestows knowledge, health and wealth.

This stone should never be given as a gift, as it will result in discord and broken relationships.

Sardonyx – The birthstone of Leo people. This gem is a popular remedy for impotence. Some believe that a sardonyx amulet could be worn to alleviate the affliction in less than a week.

Mounted in a ring, sardonyx has no power; however, worn as a pendant, the stone combats sterility. Given as a gift, the sardonyx amulet guarantees the recipient's fidelity.

Sapphire – This deep blue corundum is astrologically associated with the sign Virgo.

A sapphire pendant is a reputed cure for fever, seizures, and delusions. Mounted in a ring, the gem bestows wisdom and compassion.

When danger is imminent, this amulet reportedly takes on a chalky appearance, which remains until the hazard has subsided.

Opal – This semi-precious gem is associated with the sign Libra.

Worn as a ring, this amulet reputedly alleviates indigestion and other stomach disorders. Also, it instills tranquility and joy. An opal pendant is worn to attract happiness in love, fortune and favorable judgment in court.

The opal amulet takes on a dull gray appearance when minor illness is forthcoming. A sickly yellow hue presages injury by accident.

Topaz – This semi-precious gem is the birthstone of Scorpio people.

Some authorities insist that a topaz amulet promotes psychic sensitivity and facilitates control of destiny.

A topaz pendant reputedly bestows honor, happiness and inner peace in addition to the above benefits. Mounted in a ring, the gem insures promotion and financial success.

Turquoise – This gem, which is the birthstone of Sagittarians, has been worn in amulets since the earliest times. American Indians considered the stone sacred, and medieval sorcerers used it in various magic rituals.

Modern authorities claim that a turquoise amulet is an effective deterrent against illness and injury.

Worn as a pendant, the stone also protects its bearer from a violent death. A turquoise ring may be worn to rekindle old love affairs and obtain emotional gratification.

Garnet – This semi-precious gem is the birthstone of Capricorn people.

The stone was used extensively by early Egyptians and Phoenicians. It reputedly healed snake bite and food poisoning by absorbing alien chemicals in the blood through the skin.

A garnet pendant is usually worn to arouse the passionate love of the opposite sex and to obtain physical gratification. A garnet ring reputedly combats fear and pessimism.

Argument and eventual separation of two lovers results when garnet is given as a gift.

Amethyst – This gem, a purple variety of quartz, is traditionally considered to be the Aquarian birthstone.

An amethyst ring is usually worn for protection against sorcery and the Evil Eye. An amethyst pendant prevents depression and supposedly bestows spiritual visions.

Bloodstone – Also known as heliotrope, this variety of quartz is the Piscean birthstone.

Worn as a pendant, it prevents miscarriage and other illness during pregnancy. Mounted in a ring, the amulet reportedly promotes affluency and creativity.

Worn to bed, bloodstone may bestow pleasant dreams and clear visions of the future.

In addition to the twelve birthstones described above, there are five other gems of mystical significance which warrant consideration. These are as follows:

Amber – This gem, which has been used for magic purposes from time immemorial, is primarily a health aid.

An amber pendant reportedly cures diseases of the blood, poor circulation and prevents heart attack. Mounted in a ring, this stone combats malfunction of the kidney and protects the wearer against heat stroke and suffocation.

Beryl – This opaque stone usually comes in yellow, pink, green or white. Worn as a pendant, it promotes happy marriage and honesty. Given as a gift, it is a popular deterrent to unfaithfulness.

A beryl ring is frequently worn to insure good health during pregnancy.

Carnelian – This reddish quartz gem was highly popular in the Old World. Early Chaldeans gave the stone to enemies and thereby rendered them harmless.

According to legend, the person who wore this stone, either as a ring or pendant, became sickly and listless, thus incapable of competition.

Coral – This stone occurs in a variety of colors and is allegedly invaluable to careless people.

This amulet takes on a chalky white appearance when in close proximity with sick people. A coral ring or pendant may also be worn to promote health and wisdom.

Jade – Throughout history, this gem has been employed as a deterrent to sorcery and demonic possession. Jade is therefore considered to be one of the most potent protective devices known to mankind.

A jade pendant may be worn to achieve the above effects, a ring combats tragedy and depression.

Jet – Perhaps one of the most powerful amulets known, this lustrous black gem hold an important place in the legends of various cultures.

Medieval legend credits the jet amulet with supernatural powers. The person wearing this stone supposedly attains complete control of the natural elements – fire, air, earth and water. To accommodate this purpose, a jet pendant is usually worn.

THE INCA RITUAL OF PROJECTING YOUR SOUL BODY

This exercise will require two crystals, one somewhat larger than the other.

Hold the crystal with which you feel "friendliest" on the intuitive level in your left hand. Lightly touch the tips of the two crystals and permit the energy fields to interact.

As this is being accomplished, lean forward and breathe your intention to project your spiritual essence into the crystals. Repeat this process of intention three times.

Set the larger crystal aside and place the smaller crystal in your left hand (if it is not already there).

Place the crystal over your "third eye," directly in the center of your forehead.

You may read the following visualization, pausing now and then to reflect upon the process. Or you may wish to have a friend read the technique to you as you relax and experience the imagery.

It is also possible to record your own voice, reading this exercise into a tape recorder, so that you may play the tape back and allow your voice to guide you through the relaxation process and through the procedure.

Any of the above methods can be effective. Just be certain that you are at a time and in a place where you will not be disturbed for at least thirty minutes.

Your success in this exercise depends upon your willingness to permit a transformation to manifest in your consciousness. As an additional aid to the process, you might play some inspirational or stirring background music to heighten the effect. Be certain, though, that the music contains no lyrics to distract you.

Permit yourself to relax. . .totally and completely.

Lie back in a comfortable position and release all worries. . .all tensions. . .all problems. Let your mind float. Relax. . .relax. Take three comfortably deep breaths and relax.

Imagine before you now the softest, fluffiest cloud in the sky. See it settling down next to you as you relax. . .relax. See yourself crawling upon it to rest. . .to float. . .to relax. . .to rise to the sky and leave all your problems behind you. . .leave all your tensions behind you.

Float and drift, drift and float, rising to the sky in a comfortable slow, swinging motion. Nothing will disturb you. Nothing will distress you. No sound will bother you. In fact, should you hear any sound at all, that sound will only help you to relax. Take three more comfortably deep breaths...and relax.

You are floating up into the sky, drifting higher and higher. You feel safe and totally secure. It is impossible for you to fall. Feel peace and contentment. Drift. . .and float. Drift and float. You are entering a feeling of total peace and total relaxation.

As you are drifting and floating with your mind completely at peace, you are aware that your body has been rising higher and higher. You have been comfortably soaring through the clouds, and the higher you float, the less you are aware of any stress or tension. All of your body is completely relaxed. Your toes. . .feet. . .legs. . .torso. . .arms, shoulders...neck. . .all are totally relaxed.

You are seeing memory patterns before you. They may be the memories of another. It does not matter. You are seeing them form before you now.

The memories are taking you to a faraway place, a faraway time on the vibration of the Eternal Now. You are seeing blue, blue sky. Mountains. A city made of stone high in the mountains. An inner awareness tells you where you are. You are in Peru, high in the mountains surrounding Machu Picchu. You are remembering the ancient city.

You are remembering that you were a student there, a very special student of a very special teacher. He stands before you now in a colorful robe fashioned from the feathers of a hundred different birds.

This priest, this master-teacher, has made you his prize pupil. You, more than any of the other initiates, have responded perfectly to his teachings. When the master-teacher and other priests utter a certain sound or give you a special signal, you are able to leave your body. When the master-teacher transmits to you a secret sign, you soar free of your physical limitations. You soar high above the Earth. You soar free of Time and Space. You can go anywhere you wish – instantly. You have but to think it. . .and you will be there.

You are proud that you have become your master's special student. You are proud that of all the students in the class, you are the one who has been selected for the great demonstration.

And even now you are walking through a path, surrounded by the other students. It is night. There is a full moon. You are walking to a place where you will give the demonstration. Look around you. Remember the faces of those nearest you. Remember the faces of those standing watching you. Remember everything you see around you.

Now you are approaching the area of the demonstration. You see your master-teacher, the High Priest, is already there. His robe is blowing gently in a breeze. On either side of him stands a priest.

Twelve students step forward from the crowd and form a circle around a blanket that has been spread on the ground. You step into the circle, advance to the blanket. You take a deep breath and lie down on the blanket. You look up at the full Moon. A small cloud moves across its face. You lie quietly for a few moments, then raise an arm to signal that you are ready.

You lie there on the blanket, on your back, looking up at the full Moon. You are calm. You are relaxed. You know that when you hear or see the secret signal, you will soar free of your body. Your essential self, the REAL YOU that exists within, will burst free of the limitations of the physical body and shoot up toward the sky, toward the Moon.

The High Priest, your master-teacher, gives you the signal. NOW!

You feel yourself rushing, pushing, pulsating, spinning. . .bursting free of the body!

You, the Real You, soars toward the Moon. Down below you can see the students, the priests, your master-teacher. But your universe is only you and your spirit projection.

Go wherever you wish. You have but to think it and you will be there. . .INSTANTLY.

Think of a loved one. . .a loved one who is faraway. You have but to think of that loved one and you will be there – INSTANTLY. You will be beside that loved one INSTANTLY.

Think of a place – a city, a forest, a desert, an ocean – anywhere. Think of that place, and you will be there. INSTANTLY.

Go wherever you wish – free of Time and Space. You will return to full consciousness when you have seen what it is that you are supposed to perceive.

Peruvian Shaman, Kuichy, told the Steigers, "We are in the end times, when as prophesied, the stones will talk." Sherry Steiger 'listens' on Astral Projection rock at Machupicchu.

Chapter Eleven

THE HOPIS, PROPHETIC CARETAKERS OF THE PLANET

The Hopi mesa, Hotevilla in northern Arizona is thought to be the oldest continually inhabited village on the North American Continent. The Hopis are considered to be the keepers of Indian prophecy. They believe that as caretakers of life, humans affect the balance of nature to such a degree that humans' actions determine whether the great cycles of nature bring prosperity or disaster. Our present world is the unfoldment of a pattern which we set into motion.

We have long been compassionate to Native prophecies and attempt to share their message in our books, lectures, and workshops. In the early 1980's Sherry visited the Hopi mesa for the sacred Bean Dance Ceremony. She was invited to be the guest of the late Elder of the Hopi, Grandfather David, in his own personal kiva. Sherry was told that Grandfather David, about 108 years young, was attempting for the third time to address the United Nations with a very important message. This was crucial in carrying out the Hopis' ancient role as guardians of Mother Earth. The request was denied. This was believed by the Elders to be a vital sign.

The Hopis have been misquoted, misinterpreted, and misunderstood. Although this is certainly true of many people and cultures, we feel a great respect and love for the faith and diligence of the Hopi, and we wish to assist in getting their message out in their own way. Sherry was given the following information, some of which was prepared to be delivered to the Dali Lama of Tibet (through an emissary) and to "friends of peace throughout the world."

From the Traditional Community of Hotevilla Village, The Sovereign Hopi Independent Nation, David Monongye states: "You may ask what my own standing is. I am a religious and spiritual leader, not a

Kikmingwi, and not a political leader. I am an initiated leader of my Kiva Society in Hotevilla Village. People who hear me often tell what I say, but distort it in their own way. I get criticized for it, and this does not help our purpose. Most films also distort the true purpose of Hopi. No film to date has shown the whole truth about us. People merely coming to study humanity misrepresent us as well."

So that is why in *this* book we are going to let David Monongye's words stand as he wrote them:

> We extend our sincere blessing for the success of this occasion, and our profound thanks for your invitation to express our understanding of life on Earth, from the distant past through the days ahead of us.
>
> We understand very well that the highest way of life can only be founded upon a spiritual basis, through loyalty to the true religion of one's own tradition. For thousands of years we Hopi have followed this guideline, and we have survived to this day as proof of the truth and strength of a way of life based on spiritual forces rather than on violent forms of control.
>
> We were given our name, Hopi, for a purpose. It means peaceful, but much more than that it refers to the Creator's Law, and the way one lives within it. In our society, those who violate their customs which are seen as part of the natural order, are called "Ka-hopi," meaning misbehaved, wicked or destructive.
>
> The main Hopi villages are situated on the tops of three great sandstone mesas (plateaus), in stone houses that blend in with the mesas themselves. We grow our food in the valleys below on land that has no surface water. We depend on our prayers, which must reach the giver of rain and food in the spiritual way, without which no one could live from this land.
>
> Each village is independent, having its own religious leaders and advisors, who are responsible for the welfare of their own village. They help regulate the life of their village without dominating it through man-made laws or police. The levels of spiritual practice are similar in all the villages, but it is not the practice to interfere in the affairs of other villages. In this sense, the Hopi villages are not one nation as depicted by the Hopi Tribal Council, which is a central government designed by agents of the United States Government, and strongly dominated by outsiders, especially large corporations. We have rejected it from its beginning, and always refer to it as the Puppet Council, since it is clearly a puppet government.

No single person or group could possibly represent all the Hopi villages.

It was foretold in our teachings that someone would invent a kind of tool of government, which they could watch as one sitting on his housetop looks at something in the distance. When anyone complains about its activities, its inventors and operators would wash their hands of any responsibility by claiming that its action comes from the people it is governing. "Your own people are doing this," they would tell us.

It would be very dangerous to accept anything offered through this invented government, for although it would be claimed to work for the Hopi, in reality it will open the path by which foreign powers could control our land and take the resources.

As we were warned, the so-called Hopi Tribal Council and the U.S. Government have used the concept of central government to control the use of our land and its resources, as well as the life in our villages. It has likewise been the instrument that deals with outside businesses in our name without our consent.

So that you may understand more about our traditional way of life and its importance in the pattern of life on Earth, we offer the following observations. If you have the opportunity to see our villages firsthand, you will be able to note the changes that have recently occurred, and decide which village will be able to last through the great changes ahead.

Religion (we-me) is deeply respected by the Hopi. Its secrets are closely guarded. Only members of each religious society know the details of their respective rituals. Many of these rituals are performed in the seclusion of the particular society's *kiva*, which is a ceremonial chamber built partly underground. Each ceremony fits into an annual cycle according to the seasons. All the activities, songs, and dance movements involved in this cycle help keep the earth in balance, especially the weather conditions necessary for each season. Moisture and warmth in the spring and summer are most important for a good harvest, and for the health and happiness of all living things. The Hopi entrust their prayers to all people, as illustrated by the fact that they never charge admission fees to spectators, knowing that there may be a few among them who have good hearts and will be praying with them. The spectators who pray help the ceremony to bring an abundance of rain and food.

Spirituality is seen in four aspects: wisdom and knowledge (na-vo-de), instructions (du-da-vo), prophecy and warnings (ma-kus-da-da-vo), and beliefs (dup-tseu-nee). If a person has eyes, ears, and an open mind, it is possible to learn from written materials; but the best learning comes from the lips of wise elders and from the earth and nature. Our normal process of learning has been sadly distorted by the foreign concept of learning that has been forced upon us. Still, those who are respectful and serious about understanding the natural way can see that Religion and Spirituality are the most important ingredients for a good, long life.

Spiritual Center: The Hopi speak of living at the spiritual center of the earth. They describe the earth as a spotted fawn, each spot having a certain power. What does this mean, and what is it based on? Did we explore the earth to find this out? On what do we base our claim to all the land on this continent?

To this day, the Hopi insist that the land rightfully belongs to them. Long ago, we asked the Great Spirit, personified as Maasaw, for permission to live here with him. He is the caretaker of the land. We did not encroach upon his area as did the newcomers. He allowed us to stay as caretakers and gave us the name HOPI, entrusting us with the sacred stone tablet which is our title to the land. We hold this title only on condition that we care for it, for all people and all living things. He also gave us a warning that if we should stray from the pattern of life he laid out for us, we shall lose the use of it.

In keeping with his instructions, we migrated to all parts of the land, leaving our houses standing, and leaving rock writings and other evidence of our presence, as a symbol of our claim, and as a mysterious guardian. Thus we plant a spiritual seed at each place we rest, to reach in all directions and intertwine. The houses were always built in two or three levels. The shrines stand as a contact with their respective gods for protection.

We would stay in one place for many years, until enough food had been stored to take along on the next stage of the journey, never forgetting our mission. Some clans would travel clockwise, and others counterclockwise, keeping within a day's running distance from each other. Our destination was set before we started, at which we would meet Maasaw to receive our final instructions.

After many centuries of migration, we reached the place that is now our permanent home. Here we planted the master spiritual seed, whose roots were to join all the other roots, which would meet in this place, making the land usable. This location was originally called *Sip-oraibi*, or solid foundation.

Shrines were established many miles in the four directions, not as boundary markers, but as protectors having sacred power. Those who defile these shrines, or in any way defy the powers connected with them, thus create a curse on themselves. Thus this area was prepared as a sanctuary to enable life on earth to continue. We helped complete the spiritual center by following the directions of Maasaw.

We know that Hopi land is not the only spiritual center in the world. Other places were set aside by the Creator, through those following his directions, in other lands, to serve as sanctuaries during a time of great world-change in the future. Their roots will be found through ancient knowledge leading to those places.

It was foretold that in time the native people would stray from their original path, adopting foreign concepts. Their religious and spiritual values would be demolished, including the foundation. Their language, their culture and their identity will cease to exist. When this happens, a few remnants will remain who are possessed of the wisdom and knowledge of old. If they are fortunate enough, these few will gather together and put together the ancient knowledge which they remember, and go forth in search of the roots the Hopi laid out, until they find the master root.

What happens then will be a source of great happiness to all, especially those who have maintained the original way throughout the ages, who will be honored for accomplishing the impossible in spite of repression from outside forces. But if these last remnants of the ancient way are toppled, a very great purification by the forces of nature will be called for, in order to restore the plan of the Creator.

The Universal Plan is very clear, but people often shy away from facing or talking about the reality of it for fear of being labelled as doomsayers, and being dishonored among respectable people. But it is really the solution by which the Creator will put the world in order. The Hopi have no dispute with this plan, for we do not put ourselves above the Creator. We have no need to say exactly how the purification will be accomplished. The creator has the weapons of nature, above and beyond the armaments the humans have built for their own self-destruction. We Hopi are waiting, for we know that no human power can stop what the Creator has to do. Those of us who have served the destructive forces by our lifestyle will reap just punishment for losing sight of the bright path of the Creator. No grim fate would await us had we not acted like children and played with our toys of destruction. As it is, we must face what is in store for us.

The Hopi watch closely as each stage unfolds in the pattern of world change, knowing when to take the next action according to our instructions. So when the prophesied "gourd of ashes" was dropped on Japan, in which many people perished, the Hopi acted to bring their message to the world, to warn that no show of force must be applied. We knew that any attempt to control or conquer the world would only serve to destroy the world. This is simply the reality of life. We may use this warning to our benefit or our doom, as we ourselves choose.

Our prophets warned that at this point those who don't heed the warning and use their advanced technology to achieve greater weapons and greater control over nature would bring great harm to both land and life. These people would have no understanding, but would believe in the power of their own minds, and act as if they were some super-race. They will play the game of gaining wealth through cunning, and even treachery, using false promises in their competition for power. Who knows what they will do in their intoxicated state!

Perhaps there is still time left to re-awaken the misguided and prevent disaster. We learned from our ancestors that man's actions through prayer are so powerful that they decide the future of life on earth. We can choose whether the great cycles of nature will bring forth prosperity or disaster. This power was practiced long ago, when our spiritual thoughts were one. Will this concept still work in the jet age?

Let us not be discouraged. Let us cleanse our minds of delusion. Let us rid ourselves willingly of hate and put love within ourselves and join together with renewed faith in our Creator, so that we may be spared the destruction that results from trusting in weapons and other devices of our own minds and not forget the future of our children and those to come.

THE FOLLOWING ADDITIONAL STATEMENTS WERE MADE BY DAVID MONONGYE, IN COUNSEL WITH SEVERAL OTHER INITIATED ELDERS OF HOTEVILLA, ON THE EVENING OF OCTOBER 3, 1982, IMMEDIATELY PRIOR TO THE DEPARTURE OF THEIR EMISSARY CAROYN TAWANGYAWMA:

Now it is after sunset. It is night, and we are now talking to the Great Spirit who cares for us in the night the whole year 'round, as the sun cares for us through the day. Therefore I am sure he is listening to what I am going to say.

I hope our message reaches the right people. With the help of the Great Spirit, people will understand what I am going to say. We Hopi depend so much on Maasaw because he is the one who gave us the use of our homeland and the title to it when we first came here. We know our Father Sun will know what we say, too.

The Great Spirit has told us what we would be up against in the future. On the way, our life would become difficult. We will try to reach out to people for help, but it will be so hard for them to really help that we will have to find our own way by means of our prophecies. If we fail to get help through the communication of our message according to our instructions, the Creator's plan will be restored through wars, earthquakes, and other catastrophic events, which would purify the people.

There would be three world wars. The last one would be commanded by the power symbolized by a red cap or red cloak. When the final war comes, it will be so powerful and so sudden that our judgment could be completely paralyzed with panic. There may be no one left who understands how to regulate life through prayer, but only people who are bent on conquest, intoxicated with the conflict so much that they do not think of the lives involved. They will have so much fun shooting that nobody will be able to win. We were forewarned that even the Hopi would be pressed into serving this war. It has happened that many of us who refused warfare were hunted down and imprisoned.

It is with the realization of how real and powerful this event could become that we spread our message everywhere so that people can find the means to avert a war so great and terrible that the last spiritual people are wiped from the face of the earth.

If people recognize the truth of this, they will turn to the Hopi for survival. Some of our teachings say that people will "crawl back on their hands and knees," as they are converted, humbled by what they had had to face. Some will literally come to our land for refuge, but of course our area will not hold everyone on the world. Crawling back actually symbolizes a return to the act of living from that law which is not man-made, and therefore cannot be destroyed or changed by man. Even people in cities will notice the animals running for refuge from some event the people may not yet perceive on the horizon. Although the animals will have left Hopi land near the final stages, they will start to return for protection just before the Day of Purification.

Living things will be crying. Even a stone might be seen

rolling down a hillside, crying. In this sense, people frequently come to me asking what to do. This is not good for our people, and many of my own people hate me for receiving them. Many people come to me who are just students seeking a degree. Therefore, I always ask them what their true beliefs are, and give no information to those who are merely seeking such personal gain. Still, I must receive those who are sincere and want to face our difficult future rightly, for the sake of all life.

We must realize that this land is important. Hopi land cannot be given or sold to anyone. We must not allow the U.S. Government to explore it, for they will certainly take it over. If those involved in this takeover are not stopped through the understanding of our message about the unchangeable law of the Creator, there will be no way to prevent even the innocent from being eliminated by the wars to follow. We must consider the lives of our children.

We have heard of the protest activities against the arms race in distant places and even among Native American Groups. We approve of this growing awareness, but must emphasize that protest alone will not stop the war, any more than the weapons will. Only a life lived on the basis of the natural order of the Creator, which no person can alter, can avert the third war in the pattern of events we have studied through the centuries. In asking for help in holding on to what others have lost, we do not merely ask help for ourselves, but for all people everywhere.

The progressive Hopi (the one we call *powaka*), and the U.S. Government, try to encourage disputes among the real traditional Hopi in order to break us down and take over. By eliminating us, they can more easily explore our land and take the resources. But we will fight back even on our deathbeds. All who know the purpose of their life, and take it seriously, will fight to the death without losing their cheerfulness and hope of success.

For the Hopi, the pressure is reaching the heaviest. Our children crave what the doomed culture has to offer. We must be brave enough to criticize them for this, and keep going, even if we must turn from them and live in isolation. Later on, their own children may well criticize them in turn, and thank their grandparents who stood to the last for the way of life that can continue forever.

We Hopi have no treaty. "Treaty Indians" are very different from us. There are two paths, and one of those paths must self-destruct. To base a claim on any man-made law, such as a treaty, is to make a commitment to something that cannot last.

The Creator's law cannot be changed, so it will never break down. It can't be re-made, as with the white-man's law, even by the people, in what they think is democracy. This is why no central government can ever succeed. In this fact we can see the problem of the entire modern world. We may want freedom, but we cannot get it from any design other than the pattern of nature.

Will anyone help us keep to that pattern? It is doubtful. We have looked for many years now and tried to tell people about it, but nothing has been done to eliminate the efforts being made to prevent our children from continuing our work, and to exploit our land in spite of our true and uncompromised claim to it. When the last of us are gone, what will happen to all those living from the system man has invented? Even people in it admit that it can't last.

Our instructions were to seek help from what we now know as the White House in Washington, D.C. Receiving no redress from that source, we were to go to the "house of mica" on the eastern shore, now known as the United Nations, which we have done several times without effect. It is doubtful that the people who have finally listened to us there will help either. If they do not, there may yet be some group in the west, across the Pacific Ocean. Perhaps a court might expose the efforts to deny our freedom and deceive the world about it. If this does not succeed, it will be up to nature. Those "great waters" may actually flood across the land. There will be earthquakes, high winds, and famine, plus the wars man has prepared. When we have trampled on our original ways, this will come about.

We were forewarned that we would meet a different race that might be greedy, *lut-yawta* (literally "double talking"), who would induce us to accept favors, then turn and say, "It cost me, now you must pay." If we can't pay, they will take our land instead. Now this is happening throughout many pueblos including our own. But to this day our markings and ruins can still be seen as evidence of our claim to the land, and it is a fact of history that we have never signed a treaty. *We will never sell this land*, nor accept favors from the U.S. Government.

We just wonder why "Pahanna" does not see it this way! We still have our original stone tablet, which is the actual title to this land, and our markings stand all around as evidence!

This land provides all our nourishment. We could never sell it. Instead, we pray in our ceremonial cycles in the Kiva for all land and life. We exclude no one. We pray in the Kiva for everyone. All are free to join us in returning to the way of life which never ends, which is the way travelled by the original ancestors of everyone in this world.

According to Kuichy, Indian prophecy states that in the end times, the 'Peros' will return – an ancient community of people who are alive now, and come from the pre-Incas. They follow their sacred instruction not to mingle with and to be set apart from others.

Chapter Twelve

THE MEDICINE VISION
OF SUN BEAR

It was from Sun Bear, the Chippewa medicine man, that we first heard the expression "Walk in Balance." That brief prayer-admonition presents the crux, the essence, the ideal, not only of Amerindian Medicine Power, but of all positive metaphysical doctrines.

SUN BEAR: I think we Indians offer a pattern of balance. We may not have all the answers that pat. Or maybe we do have all the answers, but we don't have them in a manner that can be interpreted in a manner to be everything for everybody.

You know, I accept a lot of the teachings of Gandhi. I think he was a great man. I find a lot of harmony with what he taught. I find no disharmony with the teachings of the Carpenter of Nazareth, either. But I mean the *real* things he spoke of.

My medicine is for every day. It is not a thing for a Sunday treatment.

Sometimes the Nez Perce or the Klamath or some other tribe call on me to come up. If my knowledge of economic development or how to create something will be satisfying to them on that level, I am happy to make it that way. I am capable of surviving successfully on that level.

Because I have these talents, some people think that I am a promotor and so forth. But I can also take my jackknife out and skin three deer, or I can hoe a couple of acres of corn, if I have to. That is all part of the thing of it.

Everyone must learn to walk with a good balance. They must learn that I can't just give them a daily transfusion of Medicine Power. This has been the problem of a lot of people who come to The Bear Tribe saying they don't want the Establishment anymore, but they don't have the ability to balance themselves yet. This is where the big struggle is. It is a hard thing for the man who has not yet learned to carry the law within himself and to walk as a brother.

There are a lot of medicine men on the reservations across the country whose work is more with herbs and with healing. There are different degrees of medicine men. Some work with healing and some work with things of a higher nature, where they call in spirit powers to work with them.

I have to deal with the world every day. I don't feel that I have to retreat into a cave with my rattle like some of my people want me to do. I don't feel that I have to be the kind of holy man who gets out of contact with the world. I feel that a good portion of my medicine is a battle with the world as it is now, trying to rectify, trying to build things that are beneficial both for my Indian people and my non-Indian people.

When I make a prayer, when I make Medicine, I do not do it only at a certain time. I do it when it is needed. Too many white people in the System are always bugging the Lord. I have been to the meetings in churches, and I have heard them praying for television sets, for refrigerators, for new cars, I can see their picture: God is sitting up there answer-

---

Sun Bear shells walnuts as he is being interviewed. Always the pragmatic mystic, Sun Bear says, "If your Medicine can't grow corn, I don't want to hear about it."

Chippewa Medicine Priest Sun Bear, founder of the Bear Tribe.

ing all these telephone lines, sending out all the goodies. The way I have the picture, he is bursting with laughter and shaking his head.

Sometimes it is hard to be patient with those who say they want to go to the mountaintop when it is easy to see that they have not worked out a balance here because they are caught up in their own frustrations. Sometimes I tell them, "How can you go to the mountaintop when you can't solve your emotional problems? You haven't got to where you can relate to other human beings."

It is hard to have a relationship with God if you can't function on the level where you recognize that you are each others' brothers and sisters.

Those who seek a higher understanding of things must first lay a solid foundation and establish a good balance. On the basis of my experience and the experiences of my people, when you go up to make Medicine and fast to seek a vision, you are on the level of the Spirit World. If you are held back by all the worries of paying the rent and getting a new car, your mind just won't reach out.

AN OPEN LETTER FROM SUN BEAR:

"This Is A Powerful Time On The Earth Mother."

To my Brothers and Sisters:
This is a very powerful time on the Earth Mother. It is a time that we speak of as a time of Earth changes. This time has been foretold in many Native prophecies .

One of the prophecies that was given to me by the Spirit said "that the time would come when one area would be too hot, another too cold, one place too wet, another too dry, and the Earth Mother would withhold her increase,"

In 1988, three-fourths of the United States suffered major droughts; and at the same time in Europe, they had so much rain that much of their crops could not be harvested. At this time, both Russia and China are buying large amounts of grain from the U.S.A. to feed their people. Right now the world has only a 58-day, or less, supply of food. Last year was the second year in a row that the world ate more food than it produced. In 1988, the Quaker Oats Company had to buy oats outside of the United States to supply its needs.

In the state of Washington there is a prophecy that says,"that time will come when the Little Sister will speak and the Grandfather will answer, and the land will be swept clean to the ocean."

In December of 1979, a medicine brother said, "Now has

come the time for the fulfillment of the prophecy," and he moved his people over into Idaho. And in March of 1980, the Little Sister began to whisper and on May 18th of 1980, the mountain that the geography books call Mount St. Helens and the Indians of the Northwest call the Little Sister, spoke.

Some people that didn't believe the Indian prophecy are now buried beneath the mountain.

To those of us that believed, we acknowledged the Earth Mother for her cleansing and renewing process. We had planted our gardens, and we had planted a pasture in the old way of broadcasting the seeds on top of the ground, and we were praying for rain. Instead, the Great Spirit did us one better.

First, half an inch of top soil fell from the heavens, then it rained, and we had the best crop yet. The entire Inland Empire produced the best crops that year, with the replenishing of the soil.

The Grandfather who will answer is a much larger mountain, Mt. Rainier, and that answer will sweep the land clean to the ocean.

The Earth, with the help of the Great Spirit, is in the process of re-creation. Because humankind has lost respect for the Earth, it will now act to make the necessary changes, whether humankind likes it or not. The Earth is like a great big shaggy dog, and humans are like fleas in the hair of that dog, and when the earth starts shaking, they become frightened.

In 1953, I talked with Daddy Bray, a Kahuna Priest and spiritual teacher from the Hawaiian Islands. He told me that the big changes would start for the Hawaiian Islands when two volcanoes would erupt at the same time. This happened in 1984.

Some of us feel that the beginning of the time we call "Earth Changes" started in 1973. This was the year that a hundred million mice invaded Tule Lake, California, showing an out-of-balance with Nature. This was also the time when an earthquake tore half of the side of a mountain away in Montana and created what is now called Earthquake Lake. At this time some of the spiritual leaders in the country called Bangladesh, off the coast of India, tried to warn the people. They said, "Big water coming soon." But the people didn't listen to them and 500,000 people died when a big tidal wave struck the land.

Before any major destruction by the Earth there is a warning if people are willing to listen. Before any major disaster, the animals or the little insects will give you a warning. Catfish remain very still before an earthquake; cockroaches will spin around in circles; and before our volcanoes erupt in Washington State, animals show great restlessness. The Earth Mother needs to cleanse herself for her survival.

Everyone is causing pollution, from the great industries of the East, the coal burning electric plants, to our own Native American Indian people. Everyone is guilty. I go to an Indian pow-wow and I see most of my tribesmen have no respect for the Earth Mother. They throw their beer bottles all over, contributing to the great litter we leave on our reservations. We have forgotten our old laws of respect for the Earth.

Our elders should be teaching this; instead, many of them spend time badmouthing each other. We need to teach our young people respect for the Earth again so that we have a right to live upon it. We need to teach our people self-reliance. The time may come when there is no food in the supermarkets, or because of short supply, the costs may be so high that we cannot afford to buy it.

My people project to have a three-year supply of food, and we raise 70% of our own food. Teaching our people how to raise gardens is important. For the last five years we have made free garden seeds available to both Native and non-Native people, with Native people given first preference.

Getting past our food prejudices is important. If the Creator put it on the Earth, and it's good to eat, I eat it. I've eaten porcupine, muskrat, ground squirrel, prairie dog, snake, woodchuck, badger and many others and said, "Thank you, Great Spirit, that I have something to feed myself and my family."

Free yourselves of being dependent on welfare or commodity foods, because one day they may not be there.

Be sure of this, the Earth changes are happening. I feel a responsibility to make my brothers and sisters aware of this.

I saw Russia struck by major earthquakes. I told people of this five years back in 1983, and now it has happened. I also saw a map of Iran in my dreams and the word "Iran" vanished off the map. I was told by Spirit that Iran would be destroyed by its neighbors and major earthquakes. I saw up to 150 million people dying of starvation in Africa. These are all part of the earth changes.

Chapter Thirteen

ROLLING THUNDER'S
SPIRITUAL AWARENESS

We could not do a book about Shamanism without including information about Rolling Thunder, an internationally recognized inter-tribal Medicine man. It has been said by many that his powers over the elements of nature surpass any seen in recent times. He himself jokes that he has to make it rain wherever he goes to share his message – "in order to clean the polluted air" – before he speaks. His powers to make rain and thunder, to heal disease and wounds, and his abilities to transport or teleport objects through the air, as well as his telepathic abilities, have been investigated and documented by such prestigious organizations as The Menninger Foundation.

Rolling Thunder has spoken before spiritual, ecological, psychological, and healing gatherings. He has participated in conferences sponsored by the Association for Research and Enlightenment, the Menninger Foundation, the East West Academy of the Healing Arts, the Stockholm United Nations Conference of the Environment, the World Conference of Spiritual Leaders of the United Nations, and the World Humanity Conference in Vancouver, B.C., among others.

His powers as a Medicine man were described at length in the book, *Rolling Thunder* by Doug Boyd. In 1975, R.T. (as he is known by his friends and associates) gave his namesake to Bob Dylan for his Rolling Thunder Revue, and he toured for a while with Dylan, Joan Baez, and Ramblin' Jack Elliott. He has also maintained a friendship and served as spiritual teacher to the Grateful Dead and other music groups. Rolling Thunder also has Hollywood fame, as he helped to make and appeared in both of the "Billy Jack" motion picture films, one in 1972-73 and the other in 1975.

For about the last eleven years Sherry has been privileged to learn and to observe much from her friend, Rolling Thunder. In Sherry's opinion the true American Indian spiritual leader and shaman talks of the same holistic views that modern medicine is just beginning to discover. Rolling Thunder shares many things that in the past were secrets, ancient knowledge passed only from medicine man to medicine man. Rolling Thunder has declared that the time has come to reveal the prophecies and traditional teachings. Age-old Indian prophecies foretold the events of our day. These are congruous with the prophecies of many, such as Edgar Cayce, Nostradamus, and the Bible prophets. The events foretold deal with our Mother Earth being very ill, and of a breakdown in social order, among many other detailed particulars.

But more significantly for this book, the Cherokee/Shoshone Medicine shaman has a great deal to teach about life.

"I can show you how to walk softly upon the Mother Earth," promises Rolling Thunder. He says if we can do this, we will begin to both heal the planet and ourselves.

One of the most powerful and profound things Rolling Thunder says is that "the cleansing of the Earth starts with the cleansing of our minds." This credo underlies most of his teachings. "All pollution is created in the mind of modern man," he says.

"Our prayer is 24 hours a day; we don't have a one-day Sunday religion. Every day is a prayer in how you live. We have no word for religion. There is only the trail of life, and it is a circle," Rolling Thunder emphasizes. "Every thought 24 hours a day is a prayer."

"Face the sun each morning and welcome the Great Spirit; and before you enter your lodge, pay your respect to Grandmother Moon for peace of mind."

Rolling Thunder advocates giving thanks for everything. He makes prayers and offerings of thanks before taking anything from nature. Before picking an apple from a tree, taking food from his garden, or picking and gathering herbs, he offers thanks.

Rolling Thunder says: "People forget how to make a great prayer. They get demanding, praying for what they think they want. Most of their troubles, most of the bad things that are happening, come from inside themselves."

"R.T." does not make any claims for his special powers. He says, "There are many people who say I am a Medicine man, and many who say they have been healed. I do not make any claims. All power belongs to the Great Spirit. You call him God.

Rolling Thunder is known for being very outspoken and direct. He does not try to impress anyone. He tells it like it is, and states, "The Great Spirit guides me to tell people what they need to know, not what they want to know."

Because of his frankness, Rolling Thunder has been somewhat controversial, and some even regard him as militant. His views sometimes shock.

Responding to such charges, he said, "Yes, I'm a militant. So was your great healer they call Jesus Christ."

Over the last 30 years, Rolling Thunder has traveled and talked and taught and gathered and looked for what he calls, "Thunder People."

"Thunder in all the ancient mythology over there in Norway, Scandinavia, ancient Greece, and in this country, too, means `telling the truth.' `Rolling Thunder' in ancient mythology means speaking the truth. That's what I'm looking for."

He said that these "Thunder People" are going to be finding each other. People will be coming together and the Thunder People will be on a high enough level so that they can straighten out some of the things that happen – in peaceful ways.

"There's too much violence, too much destruction and violence to Mother Earth. It's getting real bad. This war they're going to have, this next war, too, is going to be the last war. World War III is coming, and that's the last war you are going to have. There will be no winners. If one of us suffers, we are all going to suffer.

"We need people, what I call Thunder People, to put their minds together as one, to believe in truth, justice, and peace. If enough people prefer peace, there will be peace. That however, is not the preference," Rolling Thunder sadly states.

"The worst enemy of all," he says, "is the violence, and you are all going to be the victims of it unless you put your minds and your hearts together."

R.T. always stresses the need for love and kindness among people: "Love is not sex or ownership. It's nothing like I see on your television where you make false promises and dare each other. Love is not made in a contract, and it does not involve possession. It is perhaps the attitude toward love that may in fact be the reason why people get to a point where they are willing to go to war."

Rolling Thunder admonishes, "White men should learn from history. Study your own history a little bit and ask yourself what you have been doing. You're fat now. You're rich. But you have not looked within yourselves. Why are we here on Earth? To see what we can do for someone else."

Rolling Thunder's attitude toward life in general is sacred. "Suicide is wrong, just as murder is wrong. The Creator meant for us to be here."

Rolling Thunder may be firm in his talk, but his language always reflects his respect for life. "There is no Indian word for `bastard'," he says, "because Indians think it is terrible to take it out on the child, or to say that the kid doesn't belong. There are also no bad names for women. Women are sacred. So clean up your language."

Rolling Thunder's strict and firm discipline and way of life are not appreciated by the weak of spirit or heart. He will not tolerate bad thoughts or language in his presence. One has to be a sincere seeker of truth and be truly willing to give up or to leave bad habits behind in order to grow and to learn the way of the Thunder People. No drugs, alcohol, firearms, cameras, or tape recorders are allowed at his lectures – and definitely not at Camp *Meta Tantay*.

Meta Tantay means "walk in peace," and that's what Rolling Thunder does on his 262 acres of arid land near Carlin, Nevada. In an effort to preserve and to revive the traditional Indian lifestyle and culture, Rolling Thunder established Meta Tantay, a non-profit corporation. Together with his dear, departed wife, Spotted Fawn, Rolling Thunder bought and paid for the land entirely with his own money in order to create a self-sufficient community where people of all races – Thunder People – live in wickiups.

"We have no mortgage payments and no property taxes. The more free you are of the tax collector and the more self-sufficient, the more freedom you have. We don't get any government help. We raise most of our own food."

People from all over the world have gone to live and to study with Rolling Thunder. In order to do so, or to get more information, one has to write and request a visit first, and "wait for an answer, before you come."

Respect for all things is practiced in the every day life at Meta Tantay. The word "respect" is more than just a word, a concept, or a thought. In the Great Spirit's way, respect is a way of life. In order to learn proper respect in the native way of life, one needs to develop the proper attitude toward all things.

Rolling Thunder teaches that this attitude develops gradually by watching one's every thought – 24 hours a day, seven days a week.

The spirit, or the way, in which one does things reflects one's true attitude and respect about many things. Everyday duties can either be seen as drudgeries or as things done as parts of a circle of life. Each part is just as important in fulfilling that circle.

Rolling Thunder affirms that is of utmost importance to do all with love. Whether planting, gathering, harvesting, cooking, serving, eating, or storing food, it is the attitude with which the task is done that determines even the affect and nourishment the food will give us.

A fervent believer in the importance of the right diet, Rolling Thunder does not allow white sugar or soda pop at Meta Tantay, because of the terrible way it affects our mind and clouds our thinking. Rolling Thunder says that one should not be so concerned with seeking "health" foods, but rather healthy foods that nourish the body, soul, and spirit. Healthy foods, in essence, he teaches, are the start of understanding what is considered "good medicine."

"Proper respect, proper attitude, and proper thinking, takes heart, faith, and patience. One needs to slow down and to go about things in a thoughtful way. The more one does anything with the proper `spirit,' the more one understands from the heart. And as one understands from the heart, one KNOWS the true meaning and importance of one's thoughts, one's attitude, one's respect in all things."

Rolling Thunder has said that the job of the Medicine man is to insure the happiness of the community. Toward this goal, he can help the human community to be healthy in mind, body, and spirit. Rolling Thunder suggests that ". . .the first step to getting well is to be honest with yourself."

Many times Rolling Thunder has stated, "There is a spiritual cause behind every sickness." Disease whether a psychological disorder, a physical malfunction, a societal aberration, or an environmental calamity, has its origins on the spiritual plane. He offers this solution as a beginning to the improvement of the health of each individual and thus the world community as a whole:

"We're going to have to change our thinking, especially about each other. . .if enough people put their minds together as one, for a good purpose, then it will come into being. If we were to put our minds together as one, there wouldn't have to be volcanoes blowing up underneath you to shake you awake.

"Anyone can be a spiritual person if they begin by disciplining their thinking. Every thought 24 hours a day should be a prayer, like my teachers taught me. The ancient ones knew this and how to heal with the mind, so begin to heal yourself by correcting your thoughts to be prayers, and you'll be making the first step toward helping the human community become healthy.

"Train yourself not to allow bad or negative thoughts, hatreds, jealousies in your mind. A warrior (whether man or woman) must be a warrior for peace. A warrior doesn't have to have a gun, because you can learn how to pray; you can learn how to sing – in a right way – and you can learn how to overcome all sickness. And that in itself is a warrior for PEACE."

This is the way of the true shaman.